I Wanna Be . . .
a Woman of God!

Also by Beth Redman

Soul Sista

I Wanna Be . . . a Woman of God!

Beth Redman

HODDER &
STOUGHTON

First published in Great Britain in 2005

3

British Library Cataloguing in Publication Data
A record for this book is available from the British Library

ISBN-13: 9780340862261

Printed in the UK by CPI Bookmarque, Croydon, CR0 4TD

The paper and board used in this paperback are natural recyclable products made from wood grown in sustainable forests. The manufacturing processes conform to the environmental regulations of the country of origin.

Hodder & Stoughton
A Division of Hodder Headline Ltd
338 Euston Road
London NW1 3BH
www.madaboutbooks.com
and www.hodderbibles.co.uk

This book is dedicated to three amazing women of God – Darlene Zschech, Nancy Alcorn and Wendy Virgo – whose lives have spurred me on more than they'll ever know.

Darlene Zschech and Nancy Alcorn both pursue Jesus with a passion, and live to glorify him day by day through their work at Hillsong and Mercy Ministries.

Wendy Virgo, whose books inspired and blessed me as a young girl, came into my life to mentor and encourage me at a crucial time.

Thank you to you all!

Contents

Foreword

In travelling the world, I meet women on every continent who are unhappy and unfulfilled. They suffer from chronic low self-esteem, and often confess to hating both themselves and the way they look. And Christian women are not exempt from the insecurity that pervades our society. Much of the blame lies with our culture's over-emphasis on looks. Image seems to be everything. We are bombarded with adverts cajoling us to buy cosmetics, clothes, and to go on sun-drenched holidays, all of which will enhance our image and make us happy. Constantly the media parade beautifully tanned and leggy women before our eyes, making most of us looking at them feel totally inadequate – and even downright ugly.

Needless to say, the image-makers are making billions

out of our obsession with our looks: liposuction, nose jobs, breast implants/reductions are all on the increase, and many women will go through untold suffering just to feel good about themselves. 'I wanna be beautiful', 'I wanna be thin', 'I wanna be tall', 'I wanna be happy', 'I wanna look like . . .' (whoever the latest icon is). Such is the frantic cry coming from the lips of many poor self-conscious, self-hating young girls. That is our culture, and it is hard to counter it.

Beth Redman points us to a better way. She is someone who understands the wavelength of today's young women. She knows what makes them tick. She has sat where they sit. She has felt their feelings and knows their struggles. From that place of understanding, she speaks the truth about our unhealthy tendencies, and encourages us to resolve the past. She shows how, with the help of the Holy Spirit, those addictive patterns can be changed, and points us to a better way – a higher goal: 'to wanna become a woman of God'.

With the help of personal testimonies and an excellent chapter on breaking the addictive cycles to which we are so prone, Beth gives many helpful pointers in becoming like the woman of Proverbs 31. There we see an uncomplicated, brave, disciplined, gracious woman whose life appears so full and worthwhile – a woman who has won the admiration of generations who long to develop just some of her attributes.

Beth presents all of us with a goal worth striving for –
to become part of a generation of women who recognise
their complete weakness, but realise God's complete
strength. Women who pursue a godly life, along with
faith, love, perseverance and gentleness; who fight the
good fight, yet remain wholesomely feminine. A generation of women who live by the Spirit, and keep in step
with the Spirit.

This is a book that will particularly appeal to young
women starting out on the journey of life and finding out
who they are in God. But it will also greatly inspire those
who have been on that road of discovery for some time,
but find themselves in need of some encouragement and
inspiration. I hope readers will enjoy it as much as I
have.

Mary Pytches

Acknowledgments

My overwhelming thanks go out to:

My incredible husband Matt – I love you absolutely, and appreciate what a truly humble, faithful man of God you are.

My gorgeous children Maisey Ella and Noah Luca – God's extravagant gift to me – and, of course, my lovely mum, Lesley.

Pete Brooks at the Church of Christ the King, Brighton, for releasing Irene Brooks's wisdom and support every Thursday for a long time. (Irene – you are wonderful!)

Terry and Wendy Virgo at NFI; Gary and Cathy Clark at

Hillsong, London; and Louie and Shelley Giglio at Passion, for their wisdom and kindness and teaching the Bible with such power and integrity.

To everyone at our new church plant called 'The Point' – such exciting times.

Natasha and Nikola Bedingfield, Jonas and Kiki Myrin, and Sarah, Aaron and Solomon – my 'God' family.

To Irene, Christy, Kimberlyn, Nancy, Sarah and Ellie, and Mary Pytches, for your invaluable contributions to the book. You are all wonderful women.

To faithful friends and sharpeners: Tim and Rach, Pete and Bee, Rach Cohn, Loretta (for always being there), Na, Anna, Miss Claire Prosser and Turid and Keir.

Finally, many thanks to the incredibly patient David Moloney and all the others at Hodder & Stoughton in London, and also to those at Regal Books, in the United States.

Once again, thank you!

1

I wanna be a woman of God

As a young girl, I was very damaged and messed up. The pain was at times unbearable – and my coping mechanisms resulted in me being an even more complicated and difficult person to be around. The grace God showed me as I grew up in these broken circumstances was the Church. No matter what sort of desert I found myself in, God always provided the river of church life to flow alongside me, bringing his comfort, shelter and love. I 'gave my life to Jesus' about ten times before I *actually* fully committed and surrendered my life to him at the age of eighteen, when he flooded my life with his Holy Spirit.

Since that day, when I fully acknowledged who he was and grasped something of the immeasurable love and sacrifice demonstrated at the cross, I've been on a mission – to know him more, to love him more, to become more like him, and to make him known to others. Even though for much of the time I was still in the same circumstances, I was not the same old me – I was a new creation. I may still have had the same reputation and labels that those in my neighbourhood and church had known me by, but Jesus had cleansed me and was continuing to change me: 'Though your sins are like scarlet, they shall be as white as snow' (Isaiah 1:18). That was just how I felt and how I still feel today.

If ever there was a dirty, messed-up sinner in need of a hope and future, it was me. The last ten years, though, have taught me that to press into God, be honest before him and confess my sin, leads to a life of wholeness and freedom. Whatever sadness, sin, suffering or crisis we may come up against, he is able to deliver, heal and restore us. The awesome God of heaven, who is surrounded by angels calling out his holy name, longs to know us and change us. Jesus – worshipped as the glorious, stunning, Saviour – changes lives and brings a hopeful and glorious future. Our God brings beauty from ashes, displaying *his* beauty within us – and even transforming other people's broken lives through us. It's a mystery. It is undeserved. It is beautiful!

At the cross, our broken past dies with Jesus and our new lives rise – just as he rose. In his light, our fractured past should no longer dictate who we are or what we will become. We don't have to inherit the sin of previous generations or carry yesterday's baggage. I know who I was before I met Jesus, and I know what sort of woman I am today; and though I'm still on the journey, I've discovered time and time again that the more I cling to him, the more he is made beautiful and glorious in my life.

So many of us women struggle with insecurity, comparison, unforgiveness, gossip, jealousy and the everyday challenges that womanhood throws at us. But when Christian women gather together, we have the opportunity to throw off these things and reflect Christ in a beautiful and glorious way. We don't have to live in the old. The new is beckoning.

I want to be a woman of God – an uncomplicated follower of Jesus who breaks free from the cycle of the past and lives a 'big life' for God. I want to leave a legacy behind. And, through this book, I want to encourage you to do the same. May these pages draw you into God's presence and cause your spirit to cry out to him. Let's not stay the same as we once were. He is calling us to dedicate our lives to him, to be women of God who bring him much glory.

Each chapter in this book is a prayer to be more like him. The chapter titles in this book are not meant to be childish 'I want, I want, I want' demands. Instead, they are the passionate prayers of a woman desperate to take hold of the things that Christ Jesus took hold of for me. This book is my prayer, a sobering look at who I am without him – and a glorious glimpse at what the future can be like because of him. God bless you on your journey, beautiful woman.

Love and grace through Jesus.

Beth xxx

2

I wanna know I'm wanted

On a beautiful day in Port Elizabeth, South Africa, in March 2000 the moment had finally arrived – my husband and I were going to be told the sex of our first baby. The doctor squirted out the jelly and jiggled the ultrasound equipment around on my stomach and told us that the wriggling, punching munchkin inside my tummy was a girl. Intuition had told me so – a precious little girl. What an absolute blessing! We rushed to the store and bought everything in pink; we just couldn't wait to start preparing properly for our daughter's arrival.

I remember the day a friend had remarked that I must be pregnant; I had left our table at the restaurant to go to the toilet *seven* times during our meal together! As my friend was a mother of three, she knew all the signs.

Matt had originally thought that we should wait till we'd been married for ten years before we had a baby, but in fact it was just two years before I became pregnant. For a long time I had dreamt of becoming a mum, but was trying to be a good and patient wife when one day God just changed Matt's heart on the matter. The next thing I knew I was taking a pregnancy test and doing the maths – I was eight weeks' pregnant. Being a sensible and practical soul, Matt decided to read the lengthy instruction booklet inside the kit before getting excited, so I was left staring at the two blue lines, overwhelmed with joy, for at least ten minutes before Matt was convinced and joined in the celebrating! We were both elated.

Both our children were planned and wanted. From day one of conception to the time of birth, they were equally anticipated with longing and love – not just by my husband and me, but by their extended family too. When they were both baptised, we invited the people who loved them the most to celebrate extravagantly. Our children are very blessed to be so treasured and loved by their family. That very fact is evident in the way they carry themselves through life and how they feel about themselves today.

Tragically, that is not how every infant enters the world. There are so many different heartbreaking scenarios into which millions of children are born each day; experiences and feelings that haunt and over-shadow a person for their whole life. Perhaps they were born at the 'wrong' time, were the 'wrong' sex, or were from the 'wrong' father. It may be that they are reminded of these facts throughout their lives. I remember one childhood friend who was brought up being told repeatedly by her dad that he had always really wanted a son. She was dressed in a football strip for parties and given goalposts and gloves for Christmas.

Obviously, there's nothing wrong with a girl not being 'girly', and being female doesn't mean you have to be pink, clean, shiny and fluffy. There are many different expressions of womanhood. There is, however, something very wrong with a girl disliking herself or her gender because she feels 'her dad didn't get what he wanted'. Sadly, in some cultures boys are a better, more valued commodity: a sign of good fortune and reward for their families. I read a recent statistic that claimed that over 60 per cent of women have at one time or another wished they had been born a man. In many places around the world today, to have a son is still regarded as an honour, but to have a daughter is seen as a misfortune. But these are certainly not the thoughts of

> I remember one childhood friend who was brought up being told repeatedly by her dad that he had always really wanted a son.

our creator God. God wants sons and daughters.

As we rejoiced and gave thanks on that day that we discovered we were expecting a girl, something even more beautiful and powerful was occurring. God was rejoicing over *his* daughter – the daughter he had known about and anticipated since the beginning of time. Of course, this extravagant declaration of love clashes with the sterile and basic facts we read about in some biology textbooks: bland text telling us we are nothing more than the coincidental result of a male sperm fertilising the egg of a woman.

A conception may be planned and wanted through love-making; or it can result from an encounter with a stranger, a miscalculation, an encounter between two people whose names are never known to the child, a horrific rape, or an incredible medical procedure in a laboratory. Whatever the emotional circumstances, the cold scientific facts remain the same: a male sperm fused with a female egg that was only the size of a pinhead, and our existence began.

We are wanted and loved, and belong to God.

As Christians, we realise that our conception is not a mere biological moment – but the unchanging biblical revelation that all of us are, in God's eyes, *pre-destined*, *planned* and *wanted*. We have a Father in heaven who was expecting us and preparing for us. We are not unloved accidents, a parent's possession, or an unwitting explosion of fate. Something much more incredible has happened to us. We are wanted and loved, and belong to God.

> 'Can a mother forget the infant at her breast, walk away from the child she bore? But even if mothers forget, I'd never forget you – never. Look, I've written your names on the backs of my hands' (Isaiah 49:15–18, *The Message*).

So what about our gender then? Can that be an accident? Textbooks tell us it is always the male sperm that determines the sex of the baby; a female egg only carries an XX chromosome, whereas a man's sperm carries either an XY chromosome, which results in a boy, or an XX chromosome, which produces a girl. Biologically, it appears to be down to the fate of the sperm on the day – but that, of course, is only if you leave our amazing Creator God out of the equation. As Christians, we do not simply live relying on what we know from science, but rather from what we know from the Creator of science – our Father God. In the Bible, God told various people the sex of their baby even before they knew they were to become parents – for instance, Mary, Zechariah, Abraham and Hannah.

So we must not underestimate how living under, and

aware of, this powerful truth can erase the pain of human circumstances, and bring a whole new security and confidence to our existence through living under the banner of our Father's love.

This truth is illustrated by this moving story from my sister-in-law Sarah Emmanuel:

I was privileged to grow up in a Christian home, believing in God and having strong Christian role models around me that I could learn from.

When I was six months old my dad died; he had committed suicide. Because of this I grew up feeling rejected in that he had chosen not to be part of my life. My mum later remarried and for a while I called that man 'Dad', but that did not work out as he ended up in prison. I would hear my friends talking about their dads and I'd long for this; but I would tell myself I wasn't good enough to have a dad. I was angry at God to begin with, but I saw how my older brother wasn't angry and he seemed happier. I realised that being angry with God was not making anything easier, but in fact harder – because I was holding all of the pain and rejection inside of me.

I remember the first time I encountered the Holy Spirit, at a youth weekend away. There, I wept for ages, experiencing God's love for me; a love I had never known before. I chose to let God in and began to be vulnerable with him, and as I did this he began to heal me and take away the pain and anger inside me. Sometimes I would close up again and get scared of letting God deep into the pain, but in times of worship I would see and experience God, and so I kept choosing to let him in and choosing to let him be my father.

God met me in times of loneliness and pain. Some days I could not bear to look at myself in the mirror; but out of those hard times he has brought good, because he has restored me.

Last year, when I got married, I walked down the aisle with my head held high, thankful for all that God has done in my life and confident in who God has made me – a daughter of the King!

3

I wanna be an uncomplicated woman

Women! We're a funny bunch, aren't we?! We have the potential to hurt and scar, as well as the ability to love and soothe, and we often seem to find 'doing life together' really tricky. For example, have you seen the discord that *can* result from women sharing houses, offices, or going on holiday together? Have you ever heard the venom of a woman hurt by another woman? Messy and frightening!

So sisters, why can't we just master the art of caring for one another, putting on love, forgiving one another, releasing one another, being pleased for one another, hurting for one another? Why do we so often end up judging one another, talking behind each other's backs, or letting jealousy take hold? What is it in our emotional DNA that causes some of us to struggle so much in this area?

Being realistic, there will *always* be the potential for catfights, gossip, insecurity and exclusivity when we women gather together. This was demonstrated on the first series of the US reality television series *The Apprentice*. In this, an equal number of men and women were chosen to live together and compete to become the boss's new executive apprentice. It certainly made for interesting viewing. The men got their suits on. The women got their claws out. Although both sexes had altercations, the men would fall out but were still able to do business and be friends, but the women would fall out and not get over it . . . *ever*! It was truly vicious.

Why do we so often end up judging one another, talking behind each other's backs, or letting jealousy take hold?

Some women become defensive, sharp and difficult – or take offence easily and become unnecessarily involved in the business of others. We may even have someone like that around us, and not know how to deal with them. It may even be that as we read this, we are aware that we ourselves have some of these characteristics.

But there is another kind of woman – one who is open

and accountable, forgiving and free. I know which type of woman it is a pleasure to share life with, and I know which one I want to be! Uncomplicated women make for much better friends. However, I also know what sort of woman I so often naturally am. The journey to being uncomplicated involves a great deal of putting ourselves under the microscope, facing up to our faults, and asking God for help. It's easier and less painful to judge and see clearly the sin and shortfalls of others, but the Scripture says, 'Search *me*, O God, test *me*' (Psalm 139:23, my italics) – not 'Search my friends' or 'Test my pastor's wife'.

How often have churches been ruined or ministries destroyed by fall-outs, disagreements and, ultimately, discord? Leaders' wives are often a fond target.

My friends Christy Nockels and Kimberlyn Hall have a powerful testimony of how God restored a devastated friendship and ministry for his glory. Here, in their own words, is the story of how God took something completely broken and transformed it with his powerful grace.

Here's how Kimberlyn tells it:

Jealousy. It attempts to kill and often does – but my story is one where good triumphed over evil. Have you ever lost a good friend or even your best friend? I have. When such a close friendship dies it is one of the most painful things – yet to have seen God breathe hope, life and forgiveness back into these shattered pieces of friendship has been one of the most beautiful.

My dear friend Christy Nockels was a precious gift from God. Our husbands (they were our boyfriends back then) had a powerful and unique ministry flowing from their hearts, leading worship together. But the more connected we all became, the more complicated ministry and friendship became. We watched the blessings of God be challenged and assailed by the enemy, as my friendship with Christy suffered blow after blow – comparisons, fear of intimacy, immaturity, lack of communication, pride and jealousy grew stronger and stronger. Then one day it all fell to pieces. The saddest day of our friendship for me was the day we sat down to talk things through – so much pain and misunderstanding. At the end of our conversation we both walked away with only the hope of distance.

I was so glad to be physically apart – but God kept my heart very much connected to his desire for restoration. Through those seven years of lost friendship, the greatest thing I learned was 'Bless her ... pray blessing on her life every time you think of her, every time you relive a memory, or wonder what she's doing, or hope to see her fall flat on her face, bless her.' These were words from Jan Bingaman, a wise friend of mine, and being so desperate, I took her advice. I guess I was hoping to receive the 'martyr's blessing' for praying for her, right? It totally backfired, and God's unfailing love rescued me from myself, and started to sow a seed of reconciliation.

God kept putting Christy and me together face to face at random times, or her name would pop up in other places, in a way I couldn't escape. Then my heart began to crack open with the birth of our first baby. While I was pregnant, word came of Christy having a miscarriage. My heart's response was unexpected – it broke. I wept and wept – though quietly, as I was still not ready to fully accept or reveal how I loved my friend dearly. Somehow in that moment my heart felt near to the grieving heart of God for his daughter.

It took one more life event – the near loss of another close friendship – to make me fully realise I was carrying a heavy load that was not mine to hold, and that I'd struggled for so long with the weight of my own emotions, yet been blinded to the feelings of my friend, Christy.

I got the chance to sit down with Christy a few months later and tell her what God was showing me. Now, I must tell you the 'what about me syndrome' was defiantly knocking at my door. Deep inside me lingered the need for God to validate the fact that we were both in the wrong, and I was not the only guilty party. But that is the beauty of God's gift – and I do believe forgiveness is a gift. He released me from holding her in debt. I needed to be responsible for my failings. I had peace that God would shine on the rest of it in due time.

Slowly but surely God provided space in our busy lives to get together and talk through our past. We sat in Starbucks for hours. My heart filled up with deep sisterhood love, and I found myself blessing and genuinely rejoicing in things I once had been so jealous of. Christy dispelled my fears of rejection with the sweetest words of harmony and unity, kindness and forgiveness – a humbling display of the beauty of God at work in our lives.

With forgiveness came freedom. I walk in relationships differently now. I stand next to Christy and sing with all my heart, praising God that he delivers and heals. Our God displays his glory when we rest in the mercy of a good relationship.

Christy's testimony is just as powerful:

The restored relationships between Kimberlyn and me is truly nothing short of a miracle. There were some attempts early on from both sides to try to restore what had been lost, but as Kimberlyn shared, it only resulted in more hurt and anger. Working out of our flesh, I think we both wanted to be the one to 'set the record straight', but I believe that God wanted to do so much in us individually and apart from one another that he completely geographically separated us! This took seven years . . .

It was so hard to watch her carry her first child as I painfully went through losing two babies by miscarriage. Many years before this I had sketched a drawing with some art pencils of Kimber and me. We both have long, dark hair, so in my sketch I drew one with a pregnant belly sitting in a chair with her head bowed and hair covering her face. The other was kneeling at the feet of the pregnant woman, her hair covering her face as well. I remember feeling awkward as I realised that I wasn't sure which one was me in the drawing. I knew which one I wanted to be! I wanted the pregnant belly first!

Years later, God brought that picture back into my heart when I had to 'swallow' the news of Kimber's pregnancy during such a painful time in my own life. I heard that still small voice, 'I want you to learn what it means to serve her, love her and get on your knees for her'. What a valuable but excruciating teaching-moment from the Lord.

I know that God had our healing years purposed and planned from the start, but I can't explain the joy and freedom of our restored friendship! How grateful I am to God for Kimberlyn's obedient heart in coming to me and letting God open a door of forgiveness to mend our friendship completely. I didn't realise until we were restored how I had allowed the enemy to put chains on me because of the hurtful things that were said between us. I was especially wounded in the area of worship.

Because of our restoration, God has released the chains, causing me to be free in his presence to truly worship him! I believe much of this freedom came from Kimberlyn pressing into places where she knew that I had been wounded by her, and allowing the Lord to undo that hurt through healing words over me. There was power in this release as she gave me her full blessing, almost a sending as a sister in the Lord to do what I'm called to do!

I can see things in Kimberlyn now that I had never seen before. I recognise her amazing gifts, rejoice in the beauty of her creativity, and I'm challenged by her walk with God. I finally feel free to bless her and fully ask God to increase his anointing and favour on her life. 'Thanks be to God, who always leads us in his triumph in Christ, and manifests through us the sweet aroma of the knowledge of him in every place' (2 Corinthians 2:14).

Christy and Kimberlyn made a purposeful choice to follow God and pursue restored friendship. Recently I've been struck by two sets of women in the Bible – Sarai and Hagar in the Old Testament, and Mary and Elizabeth in the New Testament. All of us possess the potential to live as enemies, like Sarai and Hagar, who clashed, resented and devastated each other, or we can be peace-loving and a blessing, like the cousins Elizabeth and Mary, who loved God, loved one another, and whose unity played a part in ushering in the lives and ministry of Jesus and John the Baptist.

First, let's look at Sarai's life. Sarai and her husband Abram (later known as Abraham) were unable to have children of their own. As Genesis 12 explains, they travelled and set up camp with a team of servants: Abram 'took his wife Sarai, his nephew Lot, all the possessions they had accumulated and the people they had acquired in Haran, and they set out for the land of Canaan' (verse 5).

Included in this group of people would have been the servants' wives and daughters, giving birth to a constant stream of infants. Many women today opt for careers and give motherhood a miss by choice – but in Sarai's day breeding was as much a part of life as eating and sleeping. Without children, Sarai would have stood out in an excruciating way. She may have felt others 'kindly' whispered about her and felt sorry for her. Sarai was

21

excluded not by choice, but by circumstances that she agonised over.

As any woman who gives birth will testify, without warning you are suddenly thrust into this exclusive, almost surreal club where people you had nothing in common with before are now your bosom buddies (literally!). Talk is dominated by babies, sleepless nights, feeding, and the latest trick your amazing baby has mastered. Perhaps this exclusive atmosphere would have surrounded Sarai. Each morning as she walked out of her tent there would have been the swelling bellies of pregnant women, new-born bundles, and mothers breast-feeding all around her. It would have been an agonising world to have been so close to, yet not part of; it would have driven Sarai almost to despair. Was it her fault that Abram would never have an heir? It must have appeared that way. After all, God had chosen to bless all these others, but not her. She took a deep breath and, out of desperation, took matters into her own hands:

Now Sarai, Abram's wife, had borne him no children. But she had an Egyptian maidservant named Hagar; so she said to Abram, 'The Lord has kept me from having children. Go, sleep with my maidservant; perhaps I can build a family through her.' Abram . . . slept with Hagar, and she conceived. When she knew she was pregnant, she began to despise her mistress. Then Sarai said to Abram, 'You are responsible for the wrong I am suffering. I put my servant in your arms, and now that she knows she is pregnant, she despises me. May the Lord judge between you and me' (Genesis 16:1–5).

So Sarai, exasperated at never coming up with the goods herself and feeling her solution was the only way an heir would be produced, foolishly and wearily nominated Hagar's ovaries to fulfil the role. A persuasive Sarai nagged Abram into doing what she thought was right, and then blamed him when it all went wrong.

At this point Sarai was displaying the wrong kind of strength. She was making decisions in an emotional state, which resulted in her exerting authority over her husband and, out of pain, acting without thinking. This caused the original plan God had for the couple to take on a dramatic, unnecessary twist. God had already made a promise to Abram that they would have children. Yet Sarai, out of her brokenness, was no longer able to believe that her husband had really heard God, felt her suffering and humiliation had became too much, and disillusionment set in. So she made a broken, misguided decision that only increased her pain and fuelled her anger.

As soon as Hagar became pregnant, something nasty

started to happen. No longer just a servant, she suddenly had power and control over Sarai. She dangled her pregnancy above Sarai's nose like a foul-smelling carrot. The two became arch enemies, and Sarai complained bitterly to Abram, who said: ' "Your servant is in your hands . . . Do with her whatever you think best." Then Sarai ill-treated Hagar; so she fled from her' (Genesis 16:6). Sarai's story is heartbreaking, but one that we can learn so much from. In our own lives there will be times when the things we believed God had promised do not seem to transpire. Or when something we dreamed of is taken away or denied for the time being.

Not long ago Matt and I spent a long time praying about whether or not to have a third baby. It was our dream, but we just wanted to get the timing right and, if you like, get God's permission first. During this period we were given a word that we specifically incorporated into our prayers – and we both felt it was a confirmation that the time was right.

When the pregnancy test came back positive, we were giddy with delight. All went well for the first trimester, but then at a routine scan we were distraught to be told that our little baby's heart was no longer beating.

We were so, so broken. Five months later, we were overjoyed to discover we were expecting again, but soon afterwards we lost that baby too. Right now, every time I see a pregnant woman I have to deal with the fact that it's not me. Sarai's experience has taught me to 'not be wise in my own eyes' or think God is against me. The thing that keeps me buoyant is the truth that God is for me, God is love, and God is wise. I must not write off a situation or decide what the future will look like. God is in control, holding my tears and the days to come in his powerful hands.

In spite of overwhelming pain and disappointment we must turn to God. Sarai came to the wrong conclusion that God had cancelled her heart's desire. She said to Abram, 'God has prevented me', and then tried to control events herself. This caused her life to spiral even further out of control. If we feel we are about to make a decision out of pain, then we need to meditate on God, call on him, and come to him! Psalm 4:4 tells us to 'search [our] hearts and be silent'.

> The women who know God best and make the wisest choices in times of great difficulty are those who meditate most on him.

The women who know God best and make the wisest choices in times of great difficulty are those who meditate most on him. In periods of confusion, the voice of Scripture and the still, small voice of the Father can encourage or challenge our hearts in an instant. When jealousy burns as we painfully watch someone else prospering, God can comfort us in our brokenness – and also help us to recognise the sin of envy. Turn to God, repent, and ask him to help you. God is able to change our hearts and comfort us. He is the enabling, forgiving, supernatural helper. Meditate on him.

Can a barren woman ever hope to smile at the news of another woman's pregnancy? Yes, yes, yes! His grace is enough for our deepest anguish, for the prayer we feel he's never heard, and for the sadness that for a while we must live with. In pain, don't take things into your own hands. Continue to call him your Saviour. Trust him even though your world is caving in. At times of *breakdown*, we are often nearest to a *breakthrough*.

Sarai's story also teaches us that though we suffer legitimate pain, there is no excuse for punishing another woman or starting a battle with her. Don't let the enemy allow anger to have a foothold or start a war. Just the other day, I saw a face I recognised from the past and walked over to greet her warmly. What a mistake that was! She burst into a tirade of unkind and untrue accusations. Immediately anger rose up in me. This was a character assassination, an injustice and a lie! If I had opened my mouth, I knew I would have spent the rest of my day repenting – and further still, I knew this was a battle I would not win. I listened. I turned. I walked away. Then I committed it to God in prayer. Even in agony and injustice we must recognise the potential for sin.

Hagar was only doing what her mistress had commanded her to do, but she was not peace-loving and gracious – she fought back. Instead, let's be women who even in suffering and injustice can offer love, show grace, persevere – and sometimes stay silent in the face of accusations. Only the Holy Spirit can assist us in doing that, but if we are mindful and ask him, he will help. To do this brings glory and honour to God – and breathes peace into a world of cat claws and revenge.

In contrast to Sarai and Hagar, Mary and Elizabeth show us a totally different type of relationship, as they came together in faith and hope to worship. Mary had every right to feel scared and intimidated at the prospect of being chosen at such a young age to be a mother and, most likely, face gossip and ridicule. She could never explain to those judging her whom God had called her to carry and why. Because she was just a teenager, Mary had not spent years longing for a child; she simply awoke one day to find an angel greeting her with the news of what was to come.

In contrast, Elizabeth had grown old and had longed for a child of her own over many years. She was married to Zechariah, who was a priest and a highly respected man. For this couple and their extended families, the pregnancy was a celebration.

Mary faced uncertainty and displeasure, but she chose to believe in God and rejoice. As an older, mature relative, Elizabeth could easily have felt protective and sorry for Mary (as their circumstances were so different), but as a wise woman of God she recognised Mary's baby was a blessing from God and spurred Mary to praise God and feel grateful by saying:

'You're so blessed among women, and the babe in your womb, also blessed! And why am I so blessed that the mother of my Lord visits me? . . . Blessed woman, who believed what God said, believed every word would come true' (Luke 1:42–45, *The Message*).

Elizabeth had helped Mary to praise God and exalt the privilege of her situation. Mary responded as follows:

'I'm bursting with God-news; I'm dancing the song of my Saviour God. God took one look at me, and look what happened – I'm the most fortunate woman on earth!' (Luke 1:46–48, *The Message*).

Mary and Elizabeth were an amazing combination; theirs was a friendship that glorified God and saw the privilege of their situation rather than the potential pain. They decided to look to God in praise; they chose together to view this as an opportunity for great blessing. They stayed with each other for three months, no doubt spurring each other on and praising God till their babies arrived.

This beautiful friendship between cousins Elizabeth and Mary and the antagonising break-up between Hagar and Sarai proves that a disgruntled, ungrateful heart leads to the discouragement of others. But a hopeful, believing heart leads to the hope of others. You can be an example, a witness and a stunning friend even in your sorrow and stress *if* you choose to put your hope in God, not in circumstances.

I'm not trying to promote an army of shiny, happy people – unreal about pain, unable to deal with sorrow – but instead honest, hopeful people who are real about what they feel yet unshaken by knowing God's sovereignty and presence even in times of trial. It's a choice. Our coming together can be beautiful and life-giving or harmful and wounding. And it's down to you and me to decide which type of woman we are going to let God mould us into. By making a choice to live this way, we may just start to pioneer something awesome and stunning for the kingdom of God.

So we have been set a challenge that depends on us making a lot of seemingly unnatural choices – but of course Jesus does not ask the impossible of us, or set a test we must face and perfect alone. He will help us. The most helpful and important thing we need to do is begin to increase our communication with God and our reliance on the Holy Spirit. Christ is *in* us, the hope of glory.

Reading as much of the Bible as we can; making a deliberate choice to do things differently; dying to self; choosing to go to God rather than open up to another; biting our lip rather than biting back; being humble when there is a clash of personalities – these are the marks of a woman on her way to becoming uncomplicated.

Our quest to become women of God means becoming Christ-like. We take off the old self and put on the new. It takes a strong, dependent and godly woman not to cave in. But unity and love between us could well be our most powerful weapon. As we model it and function under its banner, it will lead to strength, healing, power, security and freedom. Many of those things escape us while we stay in broken relationships where discord is allowed to live and fester. God can and will forgive and re-model us. To do this we must be honest and open – but crucially we must be humble and willing to go back and say sorry or forgive in order to go forward.

Of course our journey and desire to be united is not going to be easy, but the more we love God, the more love we will have for one another. The more we seek him, then the more we love and lean towards the things he loves – like unity, forgiveness, peace and wholeness. And we grow to become more and more like he is: compassionate, gracious, merciful and patient. Before long we'll find ourselves becoming the uncomplicated women of God we so desperately want to be.

Here is a little prayer to start us off on this journey:

Dear Father God

I am so sorry if I have ever hurt other women. I am a new creation. The old has gone, the new has come. I am sorry, Lord, and I commit myself to being an uncomplicated woman.

Help me, Holy Spirit, empower me to live this kind of life. Speak to me, and show me my weaknesses. I am turning away from the woman I can so easily be, and the wounds I have dished out and received.

With all my heart I want to be an uncomplicated woman, a good friend and an encouragement to other women. Help me to love the women you have put in my life and in my family.

Please let me become like Mary, and in your grace would you send me a friend like Elizabeth. I want to bring you glory. I want to be a blessing. I love you, Lord.

Amen.

4

I wanna know who I am

I love what are often termed 'strong' women, but there's a right and a wrong kind of 'strong'. One type brings life; the other type is destructive. Over the years I've encountered a few young women who have a passionate dream to do something for God, yet carry a dangerous attitude along with this goal. Their philosophy goes something like this: 'No one – especially not a man – is going to stop me.' You know the sort of approach – the bitter fruit of pain and brokenness. All over the world, and even in the Church, these strong yet wounded women are rising up and fighting back – but with a less than wholesome edge.

The question for all of us is this: 'Are we working out God's calling to us humbly and with reverence, gently seeking to become who he wants us to be? Or are we aggressively fighting for freedom in ways that do not match his design?'

In this chapter we are going to journey right back to the beginning, and rediscover God's original design for women. I love hearing my mum tell me all about my birth and my early years – my first moments, my first tooth, first word, and first step. But as a Christian woman, 'I wanna know who I am' in the Creator's eyes. I want to get right back to the roots of what it means to be a woman of God.

The history of women begins in Genesis. Our Creator God spoke into being the heavens and the skies, the earth, the plants and the animals. And he saw that all of it was good. But God's intention wasn't to create this beautiful scene and then just sit back in a deckchair admiring his handiwork. Our God is a God of relationship, and hadn't yet finished with 'creating':

> *Then God said, 'Let us make man in our image, in our likeness, and let them rule over the fish of the sea and the birds of the air, over the livestock, over all the earth, and over all the creatures that move along the ground.' So God created man in his own image, in the image of God he created him; male and female he created them* (Genesis 1:26–27).

That's our history – the story of how we were made in

his image, both male and female. Each sex so different, yet both made in the image of the same God.

Genesis then tells us that God said, 'Rule over the fish of the sea and the birds of the air and over every living creature that moves on the ground.' It is clear that we were created to be in partnership and to rule together with men, with the combination of both male and female gifts and personalities being equal in God's chosen package.

Elsewhere in Genesis, we read:

The LORD God formed the man from the dust of the ground and breathed into his nostrils the breath of life, and the man became a living being . . . The LORD God took the man and put him in the Garden of Eden to work it and take care of it . . . The LORD God said, 'It is not good for the man to be alone. I will make a helper suitable for him.' Now the LORD God had formed out of the ground all the beasts of the field and all the birds of the air. He brought them to the man to see what he would name them; and whatever the man called each living creature, that was its name. So the man gave names to all the livestock, the birds of the air and all the beasts of the field. But for Adam no suitable helper was found. So the LORD God caused the man to fall into a deep sleep; and while he was sleeping, he took one of the

> *man's ribs and closed up the place with flesh. Then*
> *the LORD God made a woman from the rib that he*
> *had taken out of the man, and he brought her to*
> *the man. The man said, 'This is now bone of my*
> *bones and flesh of my flesh; she shall be called*
> *"woman", for she was taken out of man'* (Genesis
> 2:7, 15–23).

Isn't it nice to know that we weren't some kind of afterthought? It wasn't that Adam tried to go it alone, but then grew lonely, and God later decided to make women! We were designed from the beginning for partnership.

When Adam was given the task of naming the animals, don't you think he noticed they were all in pairs? Don't you think he spotted that everything came in 'twos' apart from him? He may even have noticed that he had a need that had not yet been met – a need that God of course already knew about. In Genesis 2:18 we read: 'The Lord God said, "It is not good for the man to be alone. I will make a helper suitable for him." '

So that's the Old Testament story of how women came into being – but what was God's design for their role?

The passage above says our true purpose is to be a 'helper'. I didn't use to like the sound of that word. It reminded me of someone stuck endlessly in the kitchen doing the dishes! Yet if we study Scripture more closely we can see that being a 'helper' is not an insult or a description of a second-rate job, for no less than fourteen times in the Bible is God *himself* described as a 'helper'!

In fact, to be a helper is an amazing privilege, and is a calling that requires great strength of character. Yes, at times it may involve sacrificial serving and caring roles – but there is far more to this word than these sorts of responsibilities. To be a 'helper' may equally involve leadership, discipling, mentoring, teaching and decision-making. So we can see that being a 'helper' can mean a great many different roles.

Isn't it nice to know that we weren't some kind of afterthought?

The role of being a 'helper' is not just relevant in the context of a marriage relationship. We need helpers throughout the Church, and throughout the workplace too. We need women coming alongside with their creativity, their intuition and their wisdom.

There are of course some cultures and church environments that even now view women as those who help 'back out in the kitchen'. A while ago, Matt and I were hosting a meeting of leaders. I brought in some coffee and cake, but quickly realised I was not invited to join 'the boys'. The only time I was acknowledged was when the coffee had run out! My husband was really embarrassed and felt awkward that I was being treated in this way. In this day and age, it seemed really shocking.

Of course, hospitality is a great gift (and one that I am passionate about), but there is more to me, and other women, than that. I found myself wondering how these male leaders viewed me – did they think I would start crying for no reason or talking about my period?! I found myself feeling ashamed of feeling humiliated by being a woman, and saddened that I could not sit with Matt on this occasion, hearing first-hand about the exciting things God was doing. It wasn't even that I thought I *deserved* to be in the meeting – more that I was shocked to realise that even now, in my generation of the Church, women are still subject to prejudice. Sadly, there are many other women in the Church who have had this sort of experience.

Many extremely harsh things have been said about women through the ages. Plato warned that a man who lived a poor life would be reincarnated as a woman. Aristotle said, 'Woman equals mutilated male'. Josephus wrote, 'Woman is inferior to man in every way'. A Jewish man's prayer gave thanks that he was born not a Gentile, a slave or a woman; and in parts of Jewish culture, women were 'things' – they had no rights at all. They were more like a possession – like a piece of furniture – than a person. And, sadly, in the long history of the Church, women have often suffered simply because they *are* women. Even today in parts of the world, many women have no rights at all, and no choices. They cannot live under the original breath of life that says, 'Go and rule together; go and be a helper'.

Here's a quote that makes me furious from the first-century theologian Origen! He wrote: 'God does not stoop to look at anything that is feminine'. His view was that God doesn't bother with females – that he is simply not interested. In complete contrast to Origen, I have often found myself imagining that, in the moment when he created Eve, while Adam slept, the Almighty God stopped for a moment in a pause of pure delight. I remember when my daughter was born. I was stunned with delight, and in those early moments I caught her eye, and she caught mine. I just couldn't believe that this little thing lying there was my own child. My own beautiful daughter; her little toes were like my toes, and her little eyebrows were like my eyebrows.

Don't you think that's how God the Father would have looked at his precious daughter Eve that day, and every precious daughter since? Origen would have us believe that God is not interested in us – that the real occasion was the 'Adam' moment. But God did not delight over one sex more than the other. He delighted over both.

Women have these amazing origins, and yet such a broken past. What does the future hold for us? The temptation might be to say 'enough is enough' as we rise up and begin to reduce men in the same way that they have reduced us in the past. The extreme feminist backlash says, 'We don't need men', and tries to grasp back what society tells us has been taken from us. But the way of humility gives us different wisdom: God made men and women to need each other, with our contrasting strengths, personalities and gifts. We must celebrate our different qualities, thanking God for our male leaders, and realising that one sex cannot function at full strength without the other.

Over the years I've been to some women's meetings and felt almost scared of some of the women there – because on the *inside* they're rather like bodybuilders. It's easy when you've been hurt to harden yourself in order to get through life. That's the world's way, certainly, but it's not God's way. I for one don't want women to take over the world. I want to work alongside men. I want to enjoy being involved in the things that are right for me, and that use my particular qualities. I don't want to be held back, but I don't want to kick my way into freedom either.

That day back in Eden, God created a woman because that's what he chose to do. He wanted us to be part of things and very involved. He loves and cherishes his daughters – he doesn't have that 'favour thing' with boys that you may have observed or experienced with some earthly fathers. God has plans for us; his purpose is for women to live out their lives under the affection and affirmation of a perfect Father. That is God's design for women – we were created beautiful and whole, and free.

But for many of us, that is our main battle – to live life confidently in our physical shell, at ease with our inner selves. Lots of us fight against thinking we're not beautiful, not whole – and it leaves us in chains, robbed of the freedom to be all that God has called us to be.

In Genesis 1:25 it says Adam and Eve were both naked and felt no shame, but after the Fall (Genesis 2:7) the eyes of both of them were opened and they hid. Many of us today are rather similar – wanting to hide and feeling insecure as we unfavourably compare our looks with those of other women, feeling we need a tree to hide behind. God certainly doesn't want us to be victims of that particular disease of women: being ashamed of our looks, shape or size and other external things. When we feel insecure or inferior in this way, we need to *choose* to keep living in God's truth – no matter what anyone has said to us or tried to put upon us (or even those things that we may have tried to put upon ourselves). It's crucial that we focus on his truth, not that of the world.

I for one don't want to be a victim of this particular 'women's disease'. I don't want to be plagued by that sense of inferiority, or limited by a sense of insecurity. I want to be what he has created me to be. I long to be living more like that first woman he created in Eden – whole, at peace with herself, and free from all of the discontent that plagues the hearts of so many women in this world. I don't want to spend my life wishing I was someone else and that I had someone else's body.

As Christians, we don't need to buy into today's focus on physical beauty, which encourages women to have plastic surgery to eliminate their wrinkles, or change whatever it is they are not happy with. Surveys show that plastic surgery is more popular now than ever, and that a staggering 80 per cent of women want to change at least one part of their body – the most popular area being the stomach, followed closely by the breasts. Clearly unhappy with themselves, such women won't rest until that part is 'fixed' by 'going under the knife'.

But surgery cannot cure our insecurity: only Christ can enter into that deep root of body obsession and depression and bring contentment and freedom. Instead of a life focused on our faults and the shallow earthly trophy of outward beauty and body perfection, we need to radiate the inward beauty that comes from his glory.

Of course, it is good to 'look after his temple' by exercising and eating healthily, and of course reconstructive surgery after some sort of accident or illness is something totally different. What I am referring to here is the pursuit of physical perfection, and the need to change the person we were born to be because of society's stress on physical beauty. Those who have had plastic surgery for these reasons often say that it doesn't bring the contentment they had hoped it would. Frequently, once they start, they end up wanting to change all the other bits they don't like either: ears, nose, breast enlargement or reduction, liposuction – the list of options is endless.

Magazines and adverts show us beautiful faces and bodies to compare ourselves with, or we may sit on a beach in our swimwear, glancing across the sand at the girl with the perfect figure. For most of us it is almost impossible not to be aware of what we see as our own imperfections. How scary it is that there are so many surgeons ready to make so much money out of healthy but insecure women.

> For most of us it is almost impossible not to be aware of what we see as our own imperfections.

In America I heard lots of stories of fathers buying their daughters breast enlargements or nose jobs for their birthdays or graduations. This was one gift I knew my heavenly Father was not giving me permission to have (nor was my husband, by the way!), but instead he wanted to give me the gift of peace, contentment and security in my own skin – whether it be tanned, blemished, wrinkled or perfectly line-free.

Isaiah 61 speaks of all that God longs to give us in

43

exchange for all the *brokenness* we possess; verse 3 says he will 'bestow on them a crown of beauty instead of ashes, the oil of gladness instead of mourning, and a garment of praise instead of a spirit of despair. They will be called oaks of righteousness, a planting of the LORD for the display of his splendour.'

Whatever journey we are on and whatever identity crisis we sometimes struggle with, in Christ there is a new day, and a beautiful new freedom for all women.

5

I wanna be like her – part 1

'SHARPENING EACH OTHER'

One of the Bible passages that has brought incredible encouragement to my life is a really simple verse from the book of Proverbs: 'As iron sharpens iron, so one person sharpens another' (Proverbs 27:17).

The company we keep affects us, and the person that *we* are impacts on others. So if we want to sharpen, envision and challenge others, we need first to *be* iron and then *find* iron. A woman who wants to become iron is simply acknowledging a desire to grow and mature in God; iron is solid, unbendable – a force to be reckoned with.

To become strong and to have our feet on rock in times of crisis we must first and foremost cultivate a personal relationship with Jesus, and then depend on him solely as the one who meets all needs – the true source of security, identity and strength. We must also lean on God's word – the Bible itself. Throughout trauma, times of searching and when we need wisdom, storing up truth will make us more like iron.

In the book of Titus, Paul passionately writes to the Church and encourages us to 'know the truth that shows them how to live a godly life'. He carries on this theme in chapter 2 of Titus, giving more specific instructions for men and women:

> *You must teach what is in accord with sound doctrine. Teach the older men to be temperate, worthy of respect, self-controlled, and sound in faith, in love and in endurance. Likewise, teach the older women to be reverent in the way they live, not to be slanderers or addicted to much wine, but to teach what is good. Then they can train the younger women to love their husbands and children, to be self-controlled and pure, to be busy at home, to be kind, and to be subject to their husbands, so that no-one will malign the word of God* (Titus 2:3–5).

That sounds so much like the woman of God I long to be – to get on top of my current stresses, and grow in grace into a great wife, mum, friend, servant and teacher. Sometimes, to reach that place, not only do we need to get to know Jesus and his word, but we younger ones, as Paul is suggesting in the above passage, need the encouragement and training of older, more mature women. A modern word for that sort of relationship today is 'mentoring'. In other words, a sharpening relationship occurs as a more mature Christian begins to spur on and disciple a younger Christian, either on a one-to-one basis or in a small group.

FINDING A MENTOR!

For a few years we were involved in a church with a lot of young people – which often meant that even in our mid-twenties we were some of the oldest people there! Many of us would gather to sharpen one another and be 'sistas', but sometimes we desperately craved the dynamic input from the 'mothers' in God: the older women who could teach, train and encourage. In many churches today that dynamic is being stirred up and implemented, but sadly it's still not quite enough. Many women I have spoken to have longed for someone older than themselves to look to and learn from, and to gain wisdom and help from them along the way as boyfriends, engagements, church politics and everyday trials come.

This is one time when we know we women are not making 'high maintenance demands'; Titus 2 shows us that we need that mentoring relationship of training and encouragement if we are to live the godly life we desire so much.

So what do we do if we can't find this more mature woman to help us? Well, first we must deliberately become to others what we desire for ourselves, and there is something truly selfless and beautiful about this. We need to start the cycle of mentoring, training, discipling and mothering – even in our twenties and thirties. So if there is a younger Christian in your world, as the older woman you need to find a way to start loving her and spurring her on.

Many women I have spoken to have longed for someone older than themselves to look to and learn from.

Second, we need to pray for a mentor of our own. I prayed fervently for someone to help me out in the early days of being a mother – I felt just so overwhelmed with two babies under the age of two. An amazing woman called Wendy Virgo (whose books I had read as a young girl) happened to be in my church and she invited me to become her prayer partner. It was such an uplifting, inspiring season, and the fruit of those times pushed me to make sure I was being that sort of blessing to younger women in my world.

On a totally different level, it's a real blessing these days that satellite television can, for those who have it, beam into your home the most amazing and godly women. Joyce Meyer, for instance, is an incredible woman of God who has a Bible study that airs on satellite television here in the United Kingdom – with a free monthly magazine that is truly inspiring. Many times I have used her words to encourage some of the younger women around me.

Alternatively, there are many credible Christian conferences solely for women, and if you can get to these you will be really encouraged, breathed into and inspired. While these events are of course not the whole picture, personally I've found some of them to have given me the most valuable experiences in my Christian life.

If finding a mentor is something you long for in your own life, then remember that the Bible teaches us to be persistent and specific in prayer. While you're waiting and hoping, do not lose heart or feel you can't go on without a mentor; we all have the most incredible mentor of all to lean on – the precious Holy Spirit, the Counsellor, who breathes hope, joy and wisdom into us.

There are many different types of women in the Bible. We meet the manipulative, the scheming, the bitter, the deceitful ones – all those we don't want to be like. But then there are the bold, godly, wise and pure ones who we're keen to imitate – characters like Esther, Ruth, Anna and Mary. These women overcame, persevered, and glorified God. Because of that, their reputations still shine and glorify him today.

THE WOMAN IN PROVERBS 31

Another woman whose life shines and inspires is the woman from Proverbs 31. Here King Lemuel recounts the message his mother taught him: how he was wanted and loved, and how she desires for him not to waste his life on futile things, but to aspire to kindness, justice and mercy. King Lemuel's mother finishes by painting a picture of the sort of woman he should look for: the one who surpasses all other women. In character and heart, dedication and determination, this woman rises above the rest and gives all of us who are without role models a godly woman to aspire to and emulate:

> *These women overcame, persevered, and glorified God. Because of that, their reputations still shine and glorify him today.*

> *A wife of noble character who can find? She is worth far more than rubies. Her husband has full confidence in her and lacks nothing of value. She brings him good, not harm, all the days of her life.*

50

She selects wool and flax and works with eager hands. She is like the merchant ships, bringing her food from afar. She gets up while it is still dark; she provides food for her family and portions for her servant girls. She considers a field and buys it; out of her earnings she plants a vineyard. She sets about her work vigorously; her arms are strong for her tasks. She sees that her trading is profitable, and her lamp does not go out at night. In her hand she holds the distaff and grasps the spindle with her fingers. She opens her arms to the poor and extends her hands to the needy. When it snows, she has no fear for her household; for all of them are clothed in scarlet. She makes coverings for her bed; she is clothed in fine linen and purple. Her husband is respected at the city gate, where he takes his seat among the elders of the land. She makes linen garments and sells them, and supplies the merchants with sashes. She is clothed with strength and dignity; she can laugh at the days to come. She speaks with wisdom, and faithful instruction is on her tongue. She watches over the affairs of her household and does not eat the bread of idleness. Her children arise and call her blessed; her husband also, and he praises her: 'Many women do noble things, but you surpass them all!' Charm is deceptive, and beauty is fleeting; but a woman who

fears the Lord is to be praised. Give her the reward
she has earned, and let her works bring her praise
at the city gate (Proverbs 31:10–31).

As we read this passage and follow its detailed
description of this woman's nature and deeds, her
reputation shines; this is a woman with a life, a heart, a
family and a career – she's got the whole package. God
is at the centre of her life. The wisdom she has stored
up, her enduring attitude, and the kindness she has
clothed herself in means she's a joy to be around. In the
next two chapters we'll delve further into her God-given
qualities for insight and inspiration. I wanna be like her!
I've think I've just found my new mentor!

6

I wanna be like her – part 2

PUTTING THE WOMAN IN PROVERBS 31:10–31 UNDER THE MICROSCOPE!

As we put this Proverbs 31 woman under the microscope, we find many inspiring qualities that make her such a beautiful role model and woman of God:

She has no fear
In terms of anxiety and worry, many of us would love to be like this woman!

> *Verses 21–22: When it snows, she has no fear for her household; for all of them are clothed in scarlet. She makes coverings for her bed . . .*

Verse 25: . . . she can laugh at the days to come.

In Matthew 6 Jesus gives his sermon on the mount. He starts off with the Beatitudes, issuing guidelines and wisdom for right and godly living. Just after he has finished talking about the poor, he issues this powerful command:

Therefore I tell you, do not worry about your life, what you will eat or drink; or about your body, what you will wear . . . Who of you by worrying can add a single hour to his life? . . . But seek first his kingdom and his righteousness, and all these things will be given to you as well. Therefore do not worry about tomorrow, for tomorrow will worry about itself. Each day has enough trouble of its own (Matthew 6:25–34).

The woman in Proverbs 31 fully understands that the harsh conditions of winter can cause devastation to her family and her livelihood; however, she is not worried or afraid.

Even today in Britain, snow can be both chaotic and dangerous. It blocks roads; it freezes our central heating systems; and along with this can come a range of health risks. As the temperature drops and our bodies become subject to the stress of the cold, flu can spread and, in those who are vulnerable, ordinary viruses can lead to bronchitis and pneumonia. People are more likely to suffer heart attacks in very cold weather. The wise learn to take the necessary steps to get through a cold snap successfully – salt for the roads, spare electric heaters, warm clothes, and perhaps even a flu jab. The woman in Proverbs is wise enough to have made preparations for her household, should the weather turn (bed coverings and warm clothes). She makes ready – and then chooses not to fear (verse 25).

Fear and worry steal the peace and joy God has called us to live under. But can we really have peace in a world of rape, theft, assault, death, sickness, terrorism, abduction, paedophiles and every other sin and uncertainty that hangs over us daily? How can we live in peace when any moment something terrible could happen to us, or to the people we love?

> **Fear and worry steal the peace and joy God has called us to live under.**

Fear of tomorrow, though, can torment and destroy. Back in 2001, along with many others, I watched on television the terrible terrorist attacks on the Twin Towers in New York. Just three days later, I nervously boarded a plane to the United States. In those few hours on board, I realised just how much life can lead us to existing in a caged, terrified climate of 'what if?' and 'what's next?'

Jesus' teaching in Matthew 6 is not a chilled-out hippy

message along the lines of 'no worries, man', but a call to trust and seek God. The Bible tells us lovingly and with great authority that 'our times are in his hands' – and we must trust the things we hold dearest into those very same hands.

At a women's Bible study recently, the topic turned to the subject of fear and how the irrational 'what ifs?' can bind many to living a very different, small life. Since that journey in September 2001, my fear of flying had become progressively worse – to the stage, in fact, where it was stopping me going to places I felt God had called me to go. During this Bible study there was a powerful time of prayer. I really felt God freeing me and giving me back peace and confidence. Just a few weeks later, as I boarded a plane, I remembered that beautiful and encouraging line from the courageous woman in Proverbs '. . . she can laugh at the days to come'.

She is busy, diligent and disciplined

Verses 13–16: She selects wool and flax and works with eager hands. She is like the merchant ships, bringing her food from afar. She gets up while it is still dark; she provides food for her family and portions for her servant girls. She considers a field and buys it; out of her earnings she plants a vineyard.

Verses 17–19: She sets about her work vigorously; her arms are strong for her tasks. She sees that her trading is profitable, and her lamp does not go out at night. In her hand she holds the distaff and grasps the spindle with her fingers.

I used to find it hard to relate to women with such endless practical talents because I am just not like that. This woman is multi-talented; she makes clothes and bedding for her family, and she's also the budding entrepreneur because she sells the rest of the garments (verse 24). She is the ultimate practical woman! It's not simply that I can't sew or knit, but neither am I motivated to learn to do these things. Nor am I the kind of woman who is flushed with excitement at the prospect of sharing her chocolate brownie recipe with the Bible study group. I'd rather buy ready-made cakes! If you are practically minded, then you'll probably find this virtuous wife easier to relate to than I initially did. But it is not just a question of *what* this woman does, but the *spirit* in which she does it.

Whatever she does, she does it to a high standard. She seems to have a wonderful sense of balance – an eye for quality, but also a sense of responsibility with her money. If she shopped today, she would probably buy the Tesco 'Finest*' range *and* the 'Value' lines! In clothing, she doesn't 'do' just 'designer' or *just* 'budget' –

but is apparently a good steward, knowing when to 'feast' and when to 'fast'.

It's easy to envy a woman with a full life. She makes it look so effortless – she juggles commitments without looking frazzled, and seems to work hard, but without excessive striving. Many statistics and surveys show that working mothers and high-flying career women are the most stressed of all categories of people. I've met a few women who are trying desperately 'to have it all', yet finding there are not enough hours in the day. But this passage in Proverbs gives us some hope – this woman manages to be a wife, a mother, a home-maker and a businesswoman! She seems to be successful in juggling a very busy life – so what is her secret?

I believe her secret lies in the beauty of her hard-working spirit. She may be gifted as a mother and a home-maker, but my guess is her days are *not* as smooth-running and effortless as the passage seems to imply. My feeling is that her secret is that she works with great effort. She is not a complainer or a slacker. She has realised that to get through everything and run her life well, she must work hard and be disciplined.

I have worked with many wonderful Christian leaders and have come to learn that in many cases the reason they lead so well, and have been trusted with so much, is that they have learnt the art of personal discipline. It is not just what you see upfront, it is also what they have cultivated behind the scenes. Their 'quiet place' has prepared them for the impressive work that makes many feel in awe of them. How can they do that job with children? How can they run that office so smoothly? Where did that knowledge of the Bible come from? But it is usually the *unseen* hours that are the key; they use their time and lives wisely.

If my children are late for school, my Bible study rushed or unfinished, and I haven't returned people's phone calls, it is sometimes because I like to rest a little too much! I know it is my weakness, and I know it will be one of the main things that might stop me from fulfilling my purpose. If, like me, you want the big beautiful life that this woman in Proverbs has in such fullness, then we both need to recognise that it was not achieved effortlessly. She has probably sacrificed sleep, rest and relaxation, but she has gained peace, harmony, identity, godliness and a happy home.

Verse 27: She . . . does not eat the bread of idleness.

A wise woman once told me, 'mark your life by having a disciplined routine'. Her personal rule was 'in at eleven, up at seven'. In other words, be wise, sleep well, and set your alarm! Like the woman in Proverbs, we need to make disciplined choices. Laziness results in bitter consequences and a chaotic home. If we want to be trusted with much, we must adopt a hard-working attitude. God can change our hearts and our laziest habits. Just look at all that this woman achieves, simply by mastering a disciplined routine. I may feel I cannot cope, but the more I order my life, the more room there is for God.

> I may feel I cannot cope, but the more I order my life, the more room there is for God.

As in most things, though, balance of course is the key. Just as some of us have a tendency to be lazy, others will try to drive themselves into the ground with their unrealistic expectations of themselves. Be busy and organised, but don't strive to give the impression of a perfectly run life if in fact you are feeling totally burnt-out and miserable. We need to work hard, but adequate rest is just as important.

7

I wanna be like her – part 3

THE BEAUTIFUL NATURE OF THE WOMAN
IN PROVERBS 31 (VERSES 26–31)

This woman not only masters physical hard work, but she disciplines her tongue in the same way. As we know from the passage, she is both an employer with servants and a woman with children. But how does she lead those in her care? Does she rule in a fierce, dominant way? Does she have to lose her temper or deliver punishments in order to be obeyed? What is her style?

Her beautiful nature allows her to lead firmly, but in a way that is a blessing both to her family and her servants. She is very much in control, yet she leads with kindness and gentleness. She does not need to resort to anger or screaming to bring her house and her affairs under her control:

Verse 26: She speaks with wisdom, and faithful instruction is on her tongue.

Verses 28–29: Her children arise and call her blessed; her husband also, and he praises her: 'Many women do noble things, but you surpass them all.'

How difficult it is to follow someone, or to be parented by someone, whose standards are too high and harsh; the person who demands much, but issues their instructions unkindly. This woman is both easy to follow and easy to respect. She does not bark or yell commands, nor does she demand authority. She leads in a way that is a blessing to follow, in kindness and wisdom.

In Colossians 3:20 it says: 'Children, obey your parents in everything, for this pleases the Lord', and in verse 3:21 it says, 'Fathers, do not embitter your children, or they will become discouraged'. Similarly, we read in Colossians 4:1: 'Masters, provide your slaves with what is right and fair, because you know that you also have a Master in heaven.'

The woman in Proverbs 31 seems to apply both these biblical principles; she is in authority, yet easy to obey.

Not only that, but her household does not need to rebel. They are blessed by her godly approach, and as a result they esteem, love and bless her publicly. Her stunning parenting methods have brought her a great reward.

Anyone who is a daughter, parent, leader or boss knows that at times it is impossible to be listened to. I know in my house that sometimes I have to ask over and over again before the simplest task has been achieved. Each time I'm ignored, my demand becomes more fierce – and before long I'm sure I can be heard 'repeating my demand' in the next street! We may have witnessed for ourselves parenting that has been mostly made up of nagging, screeching and angry demands, but as I read this passage I realised that although shouting may get a response, it doesn't result in my household feeling loved or well led. This woman is a great example of a strong leader and a wonderful mother. The authority she has is marked by gentleness, and that is what makes her effective in her role. She is disciplining and giving instruction without scarring anyone or making them feel they have been sinned against.

> How difficult it is to follow someone, or to be parented by someone, whose standards are too high and harsh.

In our lives, we may sometimes have to parent wilful

offspring or lead difficult people. Rather than letting this ruin us, or damaging them, this wonderful woman's life shows us how to take control and lead in a calm and consistent way. Our present methods may get a certain kind of result, but I believe this woman's style of doing things is God's preferred way for us and for those under our care.

One reason that this woman has managed to achieve such a perfect style of leadership may be down to another of her beautiful attributes: wisdom. Leadership, marriage and parenting all require huge amounts of wisdom – almost supernatural wisdom! Wisdom is needed when we suddenly find ourselves out of our depth, and our brand-new 'gentle' approach quickly turns to anger and frustration. God is kind enough to offer this gift of wisdom freely – all we need to do is ask: 'If any of you lacks wisdom, he should ask God, who gives generously to all without finding fault, and it will be given to him' (James 1:5).

Many of the women who others model themselves on, and who have become icons in the world of fame and fashion, earn their living and their reputation simply by what we see on the outside – their veneer. In reality, we know nothing about their true nature or personality. We see them in magazines and films, but we do not know them. The only beauty that the media want us to see is their outward appearance – but that image will one day tarnish. What will those with little other than physical beauty leave behind?

Our friend in Proverbs 31 leaves her legacy by allowing us to know her through the Bible. She has no veneer, only depth of character and a stunning inner beauty, a kind and caring woman whose words are not her own, but learned from God. She is feminine and dresses herself in the finest linen – yet there is nothing to indicate she is materialistic or concerned with outward appearances. She takes pride in her womanhood without losing the primary concern of inward beauty. She captures the essence of woman and captivates. She is worth 'far more than rubies' and 'she brings . . . good, not harm, all the days of her life'. She is in spirit and nature everything I long to be as a woman.

> **What will those with little other than physical beauty leave behind?**

So how has she become so beautiful within and spiritually rich? Proverbs 31 ends by saying, 'Charm is deceptive, and beauty is fleeting; but a woman who fears the Lord is to be praised. Give her the reward she has earned, and let her works bring her praise at the city gate' (verses 30–31). Her God has been her resource, her inspiration, her wisdom. She has put him first, and so has become more like him. He is the one who brings about her good name and causes her to do good deeds. Just as 'the fear of the LORD is the beginning of wisdom' (Proverbs 9:10), her fear of the Lord is why she has become so greatly admired. It is her worship of God that has cultivated such a praiseworthy life.

But it may be that the standards of the woman in Proverbs 31 get your back up? Perhaps you are thinking this is just a little too sweet and perfect? The good news is that as we bring our inadequate lives before God, he *increases* and we *decrease*. We hope we will become more like her along the way, but all the time we are ultimately becoming like him if we keep his commands. So as we look at the life of the woman in Proverbs 31, let's not worship what appears to be unobtainable perfection – but instead vow to continue worshipping God, who, through his gift to us of the sacrifice of the cross, enables us to die to the old and become new creations. We are women made to bring him praise!

8

I wanna break the cycle

Many of us have a deep longing to be women of God, but before we can fully take hold of this calling, we need to break free of some of the destructive addictions and life patterns that dominate our lives – in other words, we have to 'break the cycle'. Some of us might even be living in a cycle that has been repeated throughout several generations of our family. Others of us have a certain life habit that we constantly struggle with and cannot seem to break free of on our own. The good news is that in Christ we can be free. Colossians 3:1–3 is an amazing piece of truth for those of us wanting to break the cycle of destructive ways:

> *Since, then, you have been raised with Christ, set*
> *your hearts on things above, where Christ is seated*

at the right hand of God. Set your minds on things above, not on earthly things. For you died, and your life is now hidden with Christ in God.

In other words, the good news has happened – newness and freedom in Christ. We've been raised up with Jesus. But now we must make some good choices in order to live and walk in the reality of this truth – 'set your mind on things above'. As Paul reminds us a few verses later, we take off the 'old self', and put on the 'new self' (verses 9–10).

For the rest of this chapter I'm going to leave you in the very capable hands of my good friend Irene Brooks. Irene is a trained counsellor and has a great gift for teaching in this area, as well as an excellent track record in helping many people (including me!) to talk about these issues and pray through them. Her teaching outlined below is a goldmine of biblical and practical wisdom; it contains, quite honestly, some of the most powerful insights into this area that I've ever come across. I also feel really indebted to Irene for sharing so much with us here of the problems she had prior to becoming a Christian.

So, over to you, Irene!

Irene Brooks

This chapter is about overcoming bad habits and addictions, but before we race ahead, let's remind ourselves of something very important – God loves us anyway! No matter how bound up we are in bad habits, Jesus loves us as passionately now as he did when he died for us (Romans 5:8). He is not waiting for us to 'get better' so he can love us more. We may not be enjoying all the good things he has for us yet, but his love for us is as strong and sure as it ever was (Romans 8:37–39) and he's rooting for us all the time (Hebrew 7:25). His love will help us to find our way through the most stubborn problems as long as we hang in there and keep trusting him for his help.

BAD HABITS

Any negative behaviour we can't break is a bad habit, and bad habits, if not curbed, can easily become addictions. Addictions may relieve our pain temporarily, but they always make us feel worse in the end. Jesus wants us to be free of life-controlling habits. 'But how?' we cry, reaching for the next blueberry muffin!

When I became a Christian, I was addicted to alcohol,

Any negative behaviour we can't break is a bad habit, and bad habits, if not curbed, can easily become addictions.

cigarettes and a number of other very bad behaviours. Some of my problems fell away immediately I handed my life over to Jesus, but others have taken time and hard work to overcome. Even now I know there are things in my life that God wants me to overcome.

If you are struggling with patterns of behaviour that keep defeating you, it will help first of all to understand how these patterns develop. Later, we will look at the addiction cycle and how to break out of it.

GOOD HABITS

Anyone who has learnt to drive a car, play a musical instrument (or a sport), or even to brush their teeth regularly, did so because God has built into us a wonderful capacity to form habits. A habit, roughly speaking, is any behaviour we repeat automatically without thinking about it. Obviously, some habits are good for us and some are bad – like eating too much, or shouting whenever we get angry. The good news is that because habits are learnt, they can also be *un*-learnt – and that includes even very bad, long-term habits and addictions. If a habit develops because we stop thinking about what we are doing, part of breaking a habit means learning to think again about what we *are* doing. The other part involves *choosing* to do something different. That's the best way to break a bad habit: do something that you value more instead.

'That's too easy', I can hear you say – and yes, in part, you're right. But that *is* the gist of it. As we go along, we will unpack each stage of the process so that you can better understand how to make this process actually happen. In the meantime, remember: *if you want to break a bad habit, do something you value more instead.*

When I first became a Christian my relationship with my then boyfriend abruptly died. He didn't want to believe in God and go to church – and I did. I developed a different lifestyle. Before long there wasn't room in my life for him any more, and we split up. I didn't want to hang around drinking myself into oblivion and doing things I now knew were shameful. My heart had changed, and I wanted to please God with everything within me. The more I spent time with Jesus and his people, the more I wanted to know him and please him.

Of course, these feelings are not always so strong and my motivation sinks low at times. But in the deepest places of my heart, I want God more than anything, because when I started my new life with him, God took out my old stony heart and gave me a new one that knows him, loves him and wants to do his will (Jeremiah 31:33). When we break bad habits, it's important that we do it because we love God, and not just to get out of the problems it causes us. If our hearts are not set first on pleasing God, our good intentions will not last and we will slide back into bad patterns of behaviour.

THE POWER OF THE HOLY SPIRIT

'But how?' you might ask, 'I know I love God, but I still do the things I know I shouldn't.' And this is the next key point. If we truly follow Jesus, our hearts are changed and we are filled with God's Holy Spirit. He is the 'Change Agent' God has given us. He is the One who will help us lead clean and holy lives. He is the one 'who works in us to will and to act according to his good purpose' (Philippians 2:13). Charles Wesley, the great hymn writer, put it like this: 'By faith we receive the Holy Spirit which is of God to replace the spirit of the world which is in us . . . This Holy Spirit – Christ in us . . . is that great gift which . . . God has promised . . . ' And Oswald Chambers, another great man of God, said: 'Before we can love God we must have the Lover of God in us, namely, the Holy Spirit.'

God knows our weaknesses, and it is for this very reason that he has given us the Holy Spirit to help us. Jesus told us that without him we can do nothing (John 15:5) – we cannot change ourselves, we cannot make ourselves better, we cannot overcome our weaknesses.

THE CYCLE OF ADDICTION

When a habit becomes an addiction, it means that this habit has become life-controlling to the point where it may actually threaten our lives. We often see this very graphically in the misuse of drugs or alcohol. Addictions cause ever-increasing degrees of chaos, pain and loss in every area of our lives: relationships, work, family, finances, appearance, leisure and health of body and mind. Therefore when a bad habit becomes a life-controlling addiction, we have to develop an entirely new lifestyle to break free from it. The diagram shows how the addiction cycle develops.

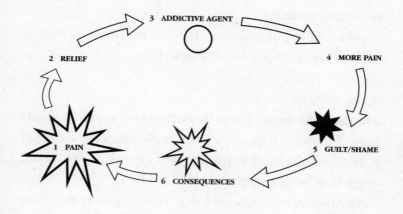

The addiction cycle starts with pain, which could be physical or emotional, or both (1). Pain makes us search for relief (2), through our favourite addiction (3). This is usually some substance or some activity that will either dull the pain, or distract us long enough to forget about it temporarily.

But the anaesthetic or distracting effect of our addiction only lasts for a short time before the pain (4) comes flooding back. It is now compounded with feelings of guilt and shame (5) as we are faced with the consequences of our behaviour (6). This usually involves losses of finances, friendship and our future, and loss of face. This leads us right back to the beginning of the cycle – and yet more pain (1). This cyclical repetition of addictive behaviour will continue unless we take drastic steps to break out of it and cultivate new, healthy behaviours instead.

Before going any further, let's have a look in turn at each of these stages of addiction.

Stage 1: Pain

Events in the present can remind us of painful incidents from the past – which is what usually kicks the cycle off in the first place. This present-day event is often called 'triggering' a past memory.

For instance, many of my own problems with depression and suicidal urges began with my angry, resentful reactions to my mother's rejection. She had a demeaning nickname for me, 'Meitjie', which is the

Afrikaans word for a little servant girl. It could have been that she meant it affectionately, but her harsh demands for me to do very difficult household chores, when I was just a small child, made me resent her deeply. A 'meitjie' was the lowest of the pile, the most despised and least desirable of the lowest of the classes in South Africa at the time. That is why I have always loathed all forms of racism, especially racist jokes.

And yes, you guessed it – I developed a great, big Cinderella complex! Oh yes, I was extremely willing to take the servant role, not expecting anything for myself, but underneath I was seething with rage and rejection. It came to a head when my first husband decided he preferred men and left me on my own with two small children. I became so depressed that I very nearly managed to destroy my life. Looking back, I now know that God saved me, even before I knew him as my loving heavenly Father. I was into Buddhist meditation at this time, and one day, while I was meditating after a very serious suicide attempt, some words came into my mind, just as if someone was speaking to me.

'Your life is not yours to throw away' were the words I heard. From that moment on, I knew I had no right to try to end my life, and somehow I managed to find other ways of dealing with the deep depressions that swept over me from time to time.

Later on we'll talk about the need to forgive the people

who have hurt us, but for the meantime the first step in breaking the addiction cycle is for us to identify painful events in our past – and the anger that nearly always lurks underneath. Paul told the Colossian Christians to rid themselves of 'anger, rage, malice, slander and filthy language . . .' (Colossians 3:8), which he said was the problem behind their bad behaviour, '. . . sexual immorality, impurity, lust, evil desires and greed, which is idolatry' (Colossians 3:5).

Dealing with anger

Christian women often deny their anger because they think it's 'wrong' to be angry. But Paul told the Ephesian Christians: 'Be angry and do not sin; do not let the sun go down on your anger' (Ephesians 4:26, ESV). In other words, we must first admit we're angry, then we must put things right with the person we are angry with that very same day. When we don't sort things out as soon as possible, anger very quickly turns into resentment and becomes a 'root of bitterness' (Hebrews 12:15). Jesus said anger stored up in our hearts is like murder (Matthew 5:21–22).

Take time to think about everyone who has hurt you and made you angry. You can express your anger by using a journal. Set a time of fifteen minutes, and write everything that comes into your mind concerning what has made you so angry. Don't stop writing until the timer rings. Don't censor what you write or check your spelling or grammar. Just write! God will not be offended by what you say – after all, he knows what's in your heart anyway. When you have finished (and it may take longer than fifteen minutes!), ask God to forgive you and heal your heart. Forgive the person or people who have hurt you. Talk to your minister or a trusted friend if necessary and ask them to pray for you.

Stage 2: Relief

We all want instant relief from pain, and we often learn to deal with our pain by copying the important people in our lives.

My own mother had a problem with depression and anger, and drank quite heavily. Consequently, that's how I too learnt to deal with my bad feelings. My dad was a very mild-mannered man, and always a safe refuge during the frequent storms in our family. Unfortunately, he never stood up for me against my mother – which I resented because she was physically abusive towards me. He would bury his bad feelings instead of tackling them directly. So I learned patterns of burying my feelings, ranting like my mother when I couldn't stuff them down any more, and anaesthetising the pain with alcohol, sexual sin and other forms of substance abuse.

Share your pain with Jesus

Jesus has not promised us a pain-free life, but he has told us he will never leave us nor forsake us (Hebrews 13:5). The writer to the Hebrews tells us Jesus has compassion for us because he has been 'touched with the feeling of our infirmities [weaknesses]' (4:15, AV), and Isaiah called him 'a man of sorrows and familiar with suffering' (Isaiah 53:3).

Here is a poem written by a young woman when she realised Jesus was with her, comforting her and sharing her pain while her mother abused her:

WERE YOU THERE? (ISAIAH 63:9)
Were you there at the first slap
When the plate crashed and the fist fell?
As I collapsed, was it your arms that I knew so well?
Were those all my tears or were they yours?
Sitting huddled in a puddle in the corner
Was it your lap I sat on?
Is that where you were?

Were you there, Abba?
When the needle pricked,
The lightning flicked,
As one hand held hair,
Did my other hand you grip?

Was your shadow present in the darkened room?
Did you see my foolishness, rejection, and sin?
Kneeling in agony, crying out in prayer,
Was your hand covering my disgrace?
Father, were you really there?

Were you there when it ended?
When hearts were split in two
Never again to be repaired
Unless they were to awaken and come to you.
Did you weep as vows were forgotten?
Jesus, was your heart breaking too?

You were there.
Soaring on your wings across the sea
I enter into a foreign, unknown land.
You release me into this place of rest
And in your grace and mercy I will forever stand.

Thank you for reminding me of your presence.
Your child.

Reproduced with permission.

When we share our pain with Jesus and experience his comfort, we find it easier to forgive and let go of the hurt. We may still not understand why God has let us suffer, but we will know he cares. The cross teaches us that he is a God who has suffered the ultimate pain, not because he deserved to, but because it was the only way to pay the price for our sin and bring us back into his loving arms for ever.

Stage 3: Addictive agent

Addictions broadly involve two groups of behaviour. First, there is *substance misuse*, which means ingesting substances that alter our mood – such as alcohol, drugs and food. Second, there is *performance addiction*. This also alters our mood, but this is achieved through activities such as over-exercising, perfectionism, being a workaholic, or over-indulging in hobbies, sports or pastimes – such as watching television, collecting, leisure pursuits, day-dreaming, religious rituals, shopping, and even swearing and shouting.

> When we share our pain with Jesus and experience his comfort, we find it easier to forgive and let go of the hurt.

The story of the lost son

Jesus told a story about a lost son (the prodigal son) that vividly contrasts these two different kinds of addict (Luke 15:11–32). The younger brother stole his inheritance from his father and squandered it on 'wild living'. In terms of putting this story into today's context, we might imagine that this involved drugs, sex and rock 'n' roll. In the original story in the Bible the younger son ended up in a distant land, alone, penniless and feeding pigs in a foreigner's pigsty – not a nice ending for a respectable Jewish boy and the son of a wealthy father! Today, he might have been a free-wheeling law-breaker who hates rules, regulations and authority; someone who would do anything to feed his addiction.

But really there are *two* lost sons in the story, although the older brother didn't leave home to get caught up in sin. We first encounter him slaving away in his father's fields, angry and alone. He has deliberately shut himself out of his father's house to avoid his younger brother's noisy home-coming. This older son is so full of rage that his father can't believe it.

'My son,' he pleads, 'we *had* to celebrate and be glad, because this brother of yours was [as good as] dead and is alive again; he was lost and is found' (Luke 15:31–32).

The older brother is actually in a far worse state than the younger one – who at least had the grace to recognise his sin and come home repentant. The older brother, on the other hand, is so deceived by his outwardly good behaviour that he can't see his need to repent. He thinks he is better than his younger sibling. But God doesn't look at the outward appearance of things, he looks at the heart underneath (1 Samuel 16:7). We see the older brother's heart in his bitter response to his father's kind invitation to join the party: it is full of jealousy, pride, rage and malice.

In some ways we could argue he is typical of some performance addicts: dedicated to looking good on the outside, with behaviour that is dutiful and self-sacrificing. But, on the inside, they may be full of rage and hurt. Sadly, the older brother in the Bible story can't see his need to repent, and the passage ends with him just standing there, still mouthing off at his father outside the house.

Neither son really knows the Father

Even though the younger son in this parable came home contrite and repentant, the Father wouldn't hear a word of his contrition and didn't want him to grovel. Today, the passage might have gone something like this:

> *'Quick!' he shouted to the servants. 'My boy's back! Send for the best take-away in town! We need champagne and party poppers. And get my best suit from the wardrobe and those new shoes I bought last week. I can't have my son walking around like a barefoot slave!'*

And to his son he might have said:

> *'And here, boy, take the family ring from my finger. No, I insist! No son of mine belongs in the servants'*

*quarters. It doesn't matter what you've done –
you're still my son!'*

Can you imagine the father's hug? Can you see the son's
astonished face as the realisation dawns on him that his
father is not furious with him? He might have said, 'I
deserve the worst, but he's giving me the best! He's not
shaming me, or punishing me for being so wicked, so
foolish. He loves me! He really loves me. I can't believe
it, I'm still his son!'

I imagine there were many tears as father and son
embraced and made their peace. And the son saw a new
side to his father – one he had never seen before.
Indelibly printed on his mind for ever would be that look
of delighted joy on his father's face in that moment when
they were re-united. He would know for ever in the
deepest places of his heart that he was loved with a love
'as strong as death', a love 'many waters cannot quench
. . . [nor] rivers wash . . . away . . .' (Song of Songs 8:6–7).

Sadly, we can't tell from the Bible story what happened
to the older son. We have to leave him there, frozen in
time, seemingly lost for ever outside of the father's warm
home and heart. To him, the father was the harsh slave-
driver, and he was the relentlessly driven son. His pride
was a merciless jailer that kept him locked out of the
father's forgiving embrace.

If you recognise yourself in this story, don't let pride

keep you locked out of the Father's forgiveness, restoration and love. If we confess our sins, God is 'faithful and just and will forgive us our sins and purify us from all unrighteousness' (1 John 1:9). That's one of the most wonderful promises in the whole Bible.

Stage 4: More pain

People often talk about the heart being layered like an onion. Sometimes it seems as if more recent pain in our lives beds itself down on to previous layers, gradually building up a wound that resonates down from the present into the deepest layers of the past.

In my own life, the rejection I felt from my mother began at birth. I was the second of twins that were definitely *not* expected! After my brother was born and my poor mum had almost died in the process, she was given the glad tidings that there was another baby in her womb, needing to be pushed out the same way – whereupon she passed out. Twenty-four hours later, she and the midwife finally got me out.

It's a long story, but there were no medical facilities where we were born in the wilds of Sri Lanka. 'The doctor thought we were all going to die,' my mother used to tell us. 'But we didn't, we all lived! But nobody knew you were there!' This last remark was always addressed at me, as if somehow it was all my fault. In my childish ignorance, I interpreted this to mean that my brother was the expected baby, while I was the nasty surprise who nearly killed my mother by being born. I felt that I really should *not* have been there in the womb (nor here in the world), and people who cause so much trouble should not be allowed to live – unless, of course, they make up for this by being very, very good, and always doing everything they are told to do.

It is unlikely that my mother intended for me to feel like this, but the difficulties I experienced with her over the ensuing years confirmed these deeply held beliefs. Of course, I was not conscious of these thoughts during my growing-up years and into my adulthood. They were deeply buried in my subconscious mind and only began to emerge after I became a Christian, and God began to heal my heart and set me free from this sense of rejection.

Everyone experiences rejection. God created us to enjoy warm, loving relationships, but Adam's and Eve's fall plunged us all into broken relationships – with God, with others, and with ourselves. Throughout, the Bible is peppered with examples of rejection. Cain, Adam and Eve's first child, killed his brother out of a sense of jealous rejection. Jacob stole his brother's rights as the firstborn and spent the next twenty years fleeing his brother's rage. Joseph was nearly killed by his brothers' jealousy and rejection, and Jesus himself was rejected and then crucified. Over the centuries, many of his followers have lost their lives because they too were 'rejected' because of their belief in Christ.

The story of the woman at the well is a good example of the layered effect of rejection (John 4:1–42). Rejected by five previous husbands and now living in sin, she went to draw water in the heat of the day when most other women would have been at home feeding their families. Her sense of racial and religious rejection keeps showing up in her conversation with Jesus.

Rejection makes people sensitive and defensive. Sometimes they become shy and withdrawn, or sharp and hostile – or even both. If you know you are vulnerable to feeling rejected, bring it to God and ask for his healing. When we look at self-image a little later, you will understand how his love heals us of this feeling of rejection.

Stage 5: Guilt/shame

Adam's first reaction to his own sin was to hide. Guilt is that awful, gut-sinking feeling that we have done wrong, and it makes us want to hide. Shame goes one step further: it is that dreadful feeling that we have failed because there is something horribly wrong with us. With shame, we don't just want to hide; we also want to get away from the eyes that see us in our shamefulness and to silence the voices that accuse us of wrong. Shame often makes us blame others – this was Adam's second reaction. Beneath his guilt and shame, Adam felt like the victim of his circumstances. So did Cain. Rejected people feel like victims.

Victims or victors?

Adam did not take responsibility for his sin. When we hide and blame others out of guilt and shame, we too are not taking responsibility for our sin. We too are acting like victims. That doesn't mean that we are responsible for the way that others have sinned towards us. God is not asking us to pretend that the wrong that others have done to us is unimportant.

My mother's rejection of me was wrong. I was a little girl who needed her love and protection. Her cruel treatment and harsh words wounded me deeply. But before I could forgive her, I had to take responsibility for my own sinful reactions: my hatred and judgments against her. Before I could move on, I had to ask God to forgive me for the hatred stored up in my heart and my rejection of my mother. Feeling rejection can make us in turn reject others, and it breaks the cycle of love that God wants us to show to everyone, even the people who have hurt us.

Honour your father and your mother

Unfortunately, my mother died before I could make my peace with her. If she were alive today, I would try to talk to her about her rejection of me and how she hurt me. I would also ask her to forgive me for judging and hating her, for setting myself against her and never letting her into my heart. But although I can't speak to her any more, God has forgiven me for my sin towards her. He has also helped me to grieve for my lost relationship with her. Now I can thank him for her. I am grateful for the gift of life I received through her, for her strength of character, her determination, her strong sense of right and wrong, and the care she gave me as a child.

Many of us have problems of resentment towards our parents for things they have done or not done. Or our resentment may be towards an older brother, an uncle, a grandfather, neighbour, teacher or gym coach, etc. We may even have been victims of serious abuse. Before we can move on, we must get rid of the hatred in our hearts.

The fourth commandment tells us to honour our father and our mother; this commandment has a pivotal place between God's commandments about our relationship with him, and the rest of his commandments about our relationships with other people. Paul said that if we honour our parents, things will go well for us (Ephesians 6:2–3). On the other hand, the Old Testament talks of a curse on those who dishonour their fathers and mothers (Deuteronomy 27:16). Bad attitudes towards our parents, whatever they may have done to us, will spoil our relationship with God and others.

Forgiveness is a hard step to take, but it is worth it. You will feel the love and peace of God like never before! Start by being honest about your feelings. Face the fact that some people have wronged you and that you are angry, hurt, disappointed – whatever is true for you. At the same time, let go of your right to judge them. The Bible says: 'Do not repay anyone evil for evil . . . Do not take revenge . . . but leave room for God's wrath . . . "It is mine to avenge; I will repay," says the Lord' (Romans 12:17–19). God is asking us to be real about the sin, but to leave the sinner in his hands. He alone knows everything, and is wise and loving enough to judge others. We are not. This is what forgiveness is all about – being real about what has happened but letting go of the right to judge.

God does not want us to put ourselves at risk by trying to befriend an abuser who has not repented.

We also need to be wise about whether it is right to seek reconciliation with the person who has wronged us or not. God does not want us to put ourselves at risk by trying to befriend an abuser who has not repented. Nor does forgiveness mean that the normal processes of law should not take place. If someone has broken the law, it may be necessary to report them.

Dealing with guilt and shame

Hiding and blaming doesn't work; it only makes matters worse. Instead, we must go straight to God with our guilt and shame. If other people have shamed us, we must forgive them and allow God to heal our hearts.

Stage 6: Consequences

Bad habits and addictions lead to multiple losses in many areas of life. It may take time for this to show, but if we sow the wind, we *will* reap the whirlwind (Hosea 8:7). Paul told the Galatians: 'A man reaps what he sows. The one who sows to please his sinful nature, from that nature will reap destruction; the one who sows to please the Spirit, from the Spirit will reap eternal life' (Galatians 6:7–8).

Let's follow the steps above and make up our minds to break out of the addiction cycle. If you need extra help, make sure you get it from someone who knows what they are doing and who will work with you for as long as it takes.

BREAKING THE ADDICTION CYCLE

Put off . . . put on

As was mentioned earlier, to successfully break a bad habit or an addiction we must not just concentrate on stopping certain behaviours. In fact, that kind of strategy can sometimes work against us. That is why dieting, for example, so often backfires. We get obsessed with eating and, guess what, the temptation gets even stronger. Instead of focusing our attention on what we should *not* be eating, we need to teach ourselves to enjoy the foods that are good for us. We can make choices to eat differently, more healthily. That, along with healthy exercise and the cultivation of other hobbies, pastimes and activities that hold our attention, will help us not to become obsessed with food fads and diets.

This is true of any bad habit we are trying to break. We need to think about the consequences of our negative behaviour and then decide instead to do other things that will be more rewarding and satisfying. Paul told the Galatians to 'put on Christ' (Galatians 3:27, AV), and the Ephesians to 'put off your old self . . . and put on the new self, created to be like God in true righteousness and holiness' (Ephesians 4:22–24). But Paul's most beautiful exhortation was to the Colossians when he wrote:

> *Therefore, as God's chosen people, holy and dearly loved, clothe yourselves with compassion, kindness, humility, gentleness and patience. Bear with each other and forgive whatever grievances you may have against one another. Forgive as the Lord forgave you. And over all these virtues put on love,*

> *which binds them all together in perfect unity. Let*
> *the peace of Christ rule in your hearts, since as*
> *members of one body you were called to peace. And*
> *be thankful. Let the word of Christ dwell in you . . .*
> (Colossians 3:12–16a).

Imagine being like that: compassionate, kind, humble, gentle, patient, forgiving, loving, peaceful and thankful! It strikes me that these qualities have a lot to do with our attitudes towards other people. Addictions, on the other hand, are all about 'me' – meeting *my* needs, fulfilling *my* desires.

A change of lifestyle

To break very serious addictions like alcoholism, continuous sexual sin, serious substance misuse, etc., we will have to change our lifestyle completely. This starts by finding a place where we have no access to the addictive substance or activity at all – at least for a while. De-tox and rehab programmes can provide a safe place to make a complete break with a destructive lifestyle. You may have to find a new place to live, a new job perhaps, and develop new friendships that have nothing to do with your addictive lifestyle. There is no easy way out of this; radical changes are needed to break an addictive lifestyle.

If this is true for you, look for the special help you

need to make a fresh start. If you belong to a Christian fellowship, I am sure they will help you all they can. But, in the end, no one can do the hard work for you. But walk in grace – and note that a *relapse* does not have to be a *collapse*. Instead, it is an opportunity to pick ourselves up, dust ourselves off, and start all over again. Work out what went wrong and get right back in there, breaking out of the addiction cycle.

Rejected people are *self*-rejecting. They usually define themselves in terms of their hurts and live out of a negative self-image. They suffer great pain, unnecessary pain. All it does is keep them locked into the addiction cycle.

To go back to my own story briefly, the fact that I ended up in a suicidal depression after my first marriage failed was largely because I believed so many lies about myself. That old rejection wound surfaced with a vengeance: 'I am such an awful woman, it is *all my fault* our marriage has broken down. Who would want to live with a woman like me, anyway? People who cause so much trouble should really not be allowed to live. The world would be a much better place without me.' Of course, I know now that none of this is true, but I didn't know it then. How tragic to think it nearly cost me my life.

It's so important that we take time to discover the negative messages that are driving us into destructive behaviour. Take a little time to think about your deepest hurts. What conclusions did you come to about yourself, other people, life and God? You may want to use journal entries in the way we suggested before, freely expressing whatever is in your heart. You may want to map out a time line of your life, draw pictures of what home felt like, or school, or that awful man next door, or the kids who bullied you in class, or the teacher who said such horrible things about you.

Then we must repent of hating, judging and rejecting ourselves. We must not reject what God has accepted, or curse what God has blessed.

Know the truth

Your identity is no longer defined by your past hurts, your circumstances, your race or colour, what others have said about you, or even what you believe about yourself. You are God's child now. He defines your identity and he has some wonderful things to say about you. You are his treasured possession, the apple of his eye. He will never stop doing you good, day and night.

It is important that we realise that, as God's children, we are secure for ever in a love that gave the best when we deserved the worst. Our worth in God's eyes is not measured by how clever we are, or pretty, or popular. Jesus gave his life for us – you and me. Our significance, destiny, importance and purpose are 100 per cent bound up in God's plans for us: plans to prosper us and not to harm us, plans to give us a hope and a future (Jeremiah 29:11).

These are the three roots of our identity: our need for security, self-worth, and a sense of significance. Rooted and grounded in the love of Christ, we can stand firm in the most difficult times and grow strong throughout the passing season of life.

Take time to think about your security in the love of God, your self-worth in the blood of Christ, and the significance of your life in the purposes that God has *for you*. Find verses that confirm these three roots of your identity. There are many. Learn them off by heart. Write songs about them. Thank your heavenly Father daily for his everlasting love, value and purposes for you. No matter what's happening in your life, your identity in God will never change. This is what the younger brother discovered in the story of the lost son. It didn't matter what he'd done, he was still his father's son.

Dealing with compulsive thoughts

Our thoughts have a powerful control over our feelings and behaviour. Paul told the Corinthians to 'take captive every thought to make it obedient to Christ' (2 Corinthians 10:5). On another occasion he told the Christians in Rome to be changed by renewing their minds. What he means is that we must take control over our thoughts and not allow them to run away with us. In some respects, our minds are like little children that have to be taught to be obedient, to behave in an orderly manner, and not run wild all over the place. He is telling the people that they must take control of their thinking so that they can live confident, productive lives in God. This is very good news for us because it means that we too can make sure our thinking is positive, faith-filled and honouring to God. Proverbs 23:7 says, 'As he [a man] thinks within himself, so he is' (NASB). If we want to live good lives, we must train our minds to agree with God's word.

Philippians 4:8 says: 'Finally, brothers [and sisters!], whatever is true, whatever is noble, whatever is right, whatever is pure, whatever is admirable – if anything is excellent or praiseworthy – think about such things.' It takes many years to train a child in the way he or she should go. The same is true of our minds. Learning God's word off by heart, thinking about it during the day and at night, singing songs full of truth, reading the Bible regularly and praying the words of Scripture back to God, are some of the ways we can get to know the word of God. If we are lazy and slack about God's word, we are like the man in Proverbs who was too lazy to mend his garden walls. Robbers laid waste his vegetable patch and spoilt his flowers (Proverbs 24:30–34).

'Catch . . . the little foxes . . .'

Sometimes we stay stuck in destructive behaviour because there are spiritual powers at work behind the scenes. This may be due to our own sin, traumas from the past, or spiritual holds that have come down to us through our family line.

I needed special prayer and help to break the power of the name 'Meitjie' over me. It had become like a curse that kept me locked into a negative self-image. If this is the case, you will probably need special help, so make sure you talk to your pastor so that he or she can direct you to someone who knows what they are doing and can help you to get free. Always remember, God wants his children to be free.

IN CLOSING

In this chapter, we have focused on the dynamics behind bad habits and addictions, how to deal with background issues, and how to break the addiction cycle. There are many specialist books and ministries that offer help in specific areas such as eating disorders, alcohol and substance misuse, perfectionism, burn-out, stress disorders, depressive states and compulsive disorders, etc. It has not been my intention to try to duplicate that kind of detailed ministry – simply to give some pointers in freeing ourselves from things that might be holding us back.

It is possible to put off old destructive ways and put on new, Christ-like behaviour. We have the Spirit of God within us to make us clean, renew us, and lead us into all truth. He knows us better than we know ourselves. And yet he loves us with a commitment and a passion that would stagger us if we could but grasp even a tiny measure of it. He is the one who breathed these beautiful words through Paul, the great apostle:

> *Now* to him who is able to do immeasurably more than all *we ask or imagine, according to his power that is at work within us, to him be glory in the church and in Christ Jesus throughout all generations, for ever and ever! Amen* (Ephesians 3:20–21, my emphasis).

Thank God that we are all caught up together in his immense care and love.

Irene Brooks

9

I wanna have a 'big life'!

Therefore have I set my face like flint, and I know I will not be put to shame (Isaiah 50:7).

I really, really want God to use my life.

A little while ago I stood in my kitchen and unloaded the dishwasher with frustration; I looked out of the window and thought of all my friends who were 'out there, changing the world' while I was 'in here' cleaning up my kids' breakfast. I prayed over and over again: 'I want a big life! I want a big life! I want a big life!' I had what you might call a 'little moment'.

In the run-up to praying that prayer I had got into a pattern of just waking up, getting through the day, and going to bed. I felt as if I were awake, but asleep. I was going through the motions without actually having a sense of purpose, destiny or vision. I had come to crisis point. My life felt small and I was without a vision.

I know God has a purpose for all of us – people for us to love, affect and reach out to. Life can be bland yet busy, or full and fulfilling. It's all about choice. I had definitely gone to sleep – awake in body, but dozing off in spirit. In that moment standing by the dishwasher I realised I was ready to dream again, to wake up and take hold of the big life that God has waiting for anyone who will surrender themselves, grasp their dreams, and make use of every waking moment to fulfil his purposes.

I could see my Christian friends taking hold of God in their own races and making a difference.

My prayer for a big life wasn't coming from a sense of boredom. I wasn't despising my life or wanting to be someone else. It was just that I realised that God had a race marked out for me and I wasn't running it. I could see my Christian friends taking hold of God in their own races and making a difference. I felt as if I'd got lost in the busyness of being a mum and the limitations that this kind of routine can bring. I'd just stopped dreaming and gone into autopilot. Every day felt like 'groundhog day' and I'd got it into my head that I was entering into my 'ineffective' phase of life. New mums, busy students and full-time workers, those who feel they only just have time to rush to church, let alone anything else, have to be aware that the more we take on, the more danger there is that we will forget to see God in all these tasks. I was missing out on the 'God-purpose' that awaits even the busiest person – what the Bible calls 'making the most of every opportunity'. I'd lost my sense of identity, and that moment at the dishwasher was when I finally woke up. I quickly finished loading the dishes in, and headed for the school gates with an entirely different attitude.

A healthy desire for a big life doesn't grow from a sense of boredom and a lack of contentment. It begins with having a vision. Just because we're busy with children or work doesn't mean we have to die to the vision. Outside of work, children or whatever it is that takes all our time, we have to ask, 'Are we fulfilled? Or are our passions and dreams lying dormant?' As we begin to open our eyes, see the need, notice people and pray, we begin once again to devote ourselves to running the race marked out for us – drawing on the power and strength of God to achieve immeasurably more than we ever could on our own. A life and a dream rooted in Christ, and seen in faith, can be lived out beyond anything we'd ever thought of or concocted for ourselves. A little person in a small town or tiny village can end up making a mark on history and affecting people's lives for ever.

Nancy Alcorn

Last year I met a remarkable woman called Nancy
Alcorn, who has recently celebrated her fiftieth birthday.
Nancy has chosen to follow a dream and allow God to
use her life to affect thousands of girls and young
women. In 1983 Nancy opened a home for broken and
hurting girls, through the organisation she pioneered
called Mercy Ministries.

A native of Tennessee and huge sports fan, Nancy had
been reaching out to troubled young women since she
was at college. A serious knee injury kept her from
playing sports at college level, but for five years she
coached young women, in the role of athletic director for
Tennessee's correctional facility for juvenile delinquent
girls.

But, as time passed, Nancy became frustrated with the
system. She wasn't seeing enough changes and thought
she might see more results if she worked with younger
children, so she asked for, and received, a transfer into
the State Department of Human Services. Here she
supervised foster-care placements in the Nashville area
of the United States, and then went on to work with the
Emergency Child Protection Services Unit, investigating
charges of abuse and neglect.

While working there, Nancy heard about a Christian

organisation called Teen Challenge and began to do volunteer work for them. In this capacity, she saw how God's word transformed people, and the positive results gave her a sense of hope that she hadn't felt for a long time. Nancy then took on the job of Director of Women for Teen Challenge, and some two years later she visited some friends in Louisiana. She soon discovered that the Louisiana area had a huge need for people to work with troubled young women, and on her return to Nashville she couldn't stop thinking about this.

She started to dream of setting up a home for women aged between thirteen and twenty-eight, where they could receive help with their various problems from trained professionals, completely free of charge, for a period of about six months. Nancy realised that many of these young women had deep-rooted emotional problems that resulted in a range of social problems, and her vision was to deal with these root problems, not just the symptoms.

So many women have been deeply wounded by incest, rape, physical and sexual child abuse, and other tragic experiences, and Nancy dreamed of creating an environment where some of these women could deal with past hurts, be relieved of guilt, and address the root causes, surrounded by the love of Christ. So began the vision of Mercy Ministries.

Nancy took her vision to the board of Teen Challenge.

They liked the idea of establishing a home in Louisiana – which would include an outreach to pregnant teenagers – but it wasn't part of their plans. So, with Teen Challenge's blessing and a $1,000 contribution, Nancy left Tennessee in January 1983 to launch a home on her own.

Initially the impact of her decision overwhelmed her. 'I was inundated with fear – I cried all the way through church on my first Sunday there,' she says. But her fear was quickly replaced with an indescribable peace. 'I believe God dropped into my heart a gift of faith, because from that point on it never occurred to me it wasn't going to work. It was just a matter of not quitting – of finding a way to do what everybody said could not be done.'

Money began to trickle in, and Mercy Ministries was finally able to open its first home. Young women came into the program from all over Louisiana and other parts of the States. The biblical philosophy she had learned at Teen Challenge was unfolding before her eyes: the power of Christ can change a life.

Eventually, Nancy wanted to expand the home, but she felt it wasn't right to take any of the government funding that had been offered to her. Instead, she believed God was asking her to rely on him to meet the need. This happened in an incredible way when Nancy found herself seated next to a businessman on a flight. She told him about the ministry, and when they landed he asked her for a brochure. A month later, the man called and said he hadn't been able to forget about Mercy Ministries. He explained that his mother had been raped and, as a result, he had been conceived. If there hadn't been a place for her to go, he would have been aborted. He went on to ask her how much she needed for the new home. When she told him she needed $150,000, he said instantly, 'You've got it'. He gave the money anonymously, with no strings attached.

In 1990, Nancy felt God was calling her back to Nashville to establish a home there. So she moved, and for five years she travelled extensively to help to raise funds for a new home for forty women. Her dream became a reality in 1995 when a $2million facility was completed – entirely debt-free.

Since then, Mercy Ministries has opened two homes in Sydney in Australia and is planning a third. In addition, Mercy is looking for property in New Zealand, and is also currently renovating a home in St Louis that was donated by Joyce Meyer Ministries. Other homes are in the United Kingdom, Los Angeles and Houston.

Every day over 7 million girls in the United States struggle with eating disorders; 2,795 become pregnant; 15,000 begin using drugs; and 11 commit suicide. Nancy Alcorn saw this need, and dedicated her life to living the big life God had in mind for her, fulfilling the vision. Her faithfulness and obedience has made a permanent difference to thousands of girls' lives and their futures.

Mother Teresa

Another woman who said yes to a big life, and demonstrated faithfulness and obedience in a powerful, extravagant way was Mother Teresa. As I read her life story it struck me that she did not have to be obedient to the call God placed upon her life. But she made herself available, boarded a train alone for Calcutta, and took up her cross and followed Jesus. From that moment on her love for Jesus propelled her into an ever-growing vision for the poor of that city. It must have been frightening at times, isolating and infuriating – but this was it.

On one occasion a cynical press reporter asked her, 'But Mother Teresa, isn't all you are doing just a drop in the ocean?' 'Yes,' she replied, 'but the ocean is made up of many drops.' A fantastic response, which drives home the point that the smallness we feel about our lives comes from within. Here was the 'big life', one that made a difference to thousands of people's existences. Mother Teresa comforted the lives of countless people, and nursed many into the arms of Jesus for all eternity.

How are we going to use our lives? What are your dreams? The lives of these two women, Nancy Alcorn and Mother Teresa, show us that God takes the faithful dreamer and pours out the extraordinary blessing of a full life – a life that gives glory to Jesus and extravagant encouragement to others.

> *For we are God's workmanship, created in Christ Jesus to do good works, which God* prepared in advance for us to do (Ephesians 2:10, my emphasis).

> *Now to him who is able to do immeasurably more than all we ask or imagine, according to his power that is at work within us, to him be glory in the church and in Christ Jesus throughout all generations, for ever and ever! Amen* (Ephesians 3:20–21).

Jesus created and designed each of us with a destiny, a purpose and a plan. We have a simple choice to make: to live the *full life* he's prepared for us, or to take a smaller, less risky life. A big life is available to all believers, but is usually marked by some costly characteristics: an unyielding devotion to Christ, a passion to make a difference, and the ability to sow and persevere in the most trying of situations. Ironically, some of the fruit of having a big life can actually make our day-to-day existence feel small and uninteresting, as the big life may involve a lot of work and lots of waiting.

I recently read a story in a national newspaper about a woman in her thirties who dreamed of having a baby, yet she suddenly felt hemmed in and dissatisfied when her little bundle arrived. 'Babies are boring' the article declared. This was not the experience she had expected it to be. The nappies, crying and endless feeding quickly became tedious and distasteful. She was not able to have the vision or the perseverance to stick it out till the next stage – to work for the dream, to wait a bit longer for it to develop and mature. So she packed her baby off to a nursery in search of a bigger life.

How are we going to use our lives? What are your dreams?

The very next day there was another article written by several mums in response to her outburst. A few vehemently disagreed with her views, but many, many more women agreed. Words like 'unstimulated', 'depressed', 'despondent' and 'disillusioned' filled the page; these women had run out of vision and no longer had the energy to nurture and work for the dream.

But for Christians, in all areas of life (not just motherhood), perseverance and focusing on the Creator of our vision will be the key to us holding out when times are tough, and pressing on to receive the promise.

. . . let us run with perseverance the race marked out for us. Let us fix our eyes on Jesus, the author and perfecter of our faith . . . (Hebrews 12:1–2).

God has a race marked out for each one of us. We're all running in the same direction, but no one else can have our lane or the opportunities God is giving us. We are unique. In Christianity there are no clones! Recently I listened with passion and enthusiasm to a woman called Donna Crouch, speaking at a conference in London. The title of her talk was 'Escaping a small life – stir up the woman born for a great cause'. In *The Message*, the version of 2 Corinthians 6:11–13 is as follows:

Dear, dear Corinthians, I can't tell you how much I long for you to enter this wide-open, spacious life. We didn't fence you in. The smallness you feel comes from within you. Your lives aren't small, but you're living them in a small way. I'm speaking as plainly as I can and with great affection. Open up your lives. Live openly and expansively!

This is the path that leads to an extraordinary life. Sometimes the journey may be hard, boring, or even lonely – and we think we've missed out on having a full life. But when we get a glimpse of God's perspective, we soon begin to realise that even the 'small bits' are a crucial part of embracing the big, marvellous life God has given us.

I have always had a massive heart for young women, and five years ago I was privileged to be offered the job of running an organisation called Soul Sista. I really wanted to see these girls know Jesus more deeply, and be set free from the many burdens and lies that held them back from living a full life before him. We set up conferences and training days, but I realised early on that seeing these girls grow and be healed would be just 5 per cent of my job. To make it happen would require 95 per cent hard work, organisation and administration (as well as maintaining my first priorities, which were running my home and looking after our small children full time). To realise the dream took a lot of sacrifice and hard work! But did I want the big life or not?

Sometimes I wanted to escape the seeming smallness of my everyday routine – washing, ironing, cleaning, making phone calls, organising paperwork, arranging merchandise – and escape to a more glamorous life for the day. But I also knew that changing my *attitude* was the key to finding and fulfilling my purpose. We can either be prepared to work for the dream by waking up tomorrow with a sense of anticipation and gratitude, walking into our world and embracing all that's ahead of us, or simply miss it by grumbling at the potentially unexciting events of the day and settling for life without a dream.

I learnt so much from Nancy Alcorn's story – her vision to set up another home in Nashville. Did she receive the dream straight away? No – she travelled extensively for five years before the funds were raised and the house in Nashville was built. The more vision she had, the more she had to work and wait for the dream.

For new mums, busy students, stressed professionals, and any other category that you might find yourself in – whatever our particular challenge looks like, for most of us there will be times of excruciating perseverance. We have to strive not to get discouraged. Hebrews 12 encourages us to look back at all the faithful runners from Hebrews 11 who kept going to win the prize; remember them, remember Nancy, and in times of endurance hold on to Jesus!

An extraordinary life comes with a price tag, and if we really want to live life to the fullest in Christ, it will take discipline, vision and endurance. I quite like the phrase 'make hard work your slave'. Whether our particular race is run in the home, the office, or at the college desk, there will be a cost involved. For me, I know there is no point in being dramatic and whiny when it gets to 10 p.m. and I've got packed lunches to make, washing to be done, or a Bible study to prepare. It *is* hard work, but we are brave women and we can multi-task! We can shove a load in the washing machine, butter a sandwich, and take stuff out of the dishwasher all at the same time! Let's not waste time and energy being dramatic and frustrated – let's just get on with it with a grateful attitude and realise this busyness is part of the big life we asked for. Habakkuk 2:2 encourages us to write down the vision. Proverbs 29:18 tells us 'without a vision the people perish'. If we don't have a vision or a dream, we are not living our God life to the full. If we think of ourselves as insignificant cogs, then we have no vision. We've got to know who we are and what we're for.

There is a time for everything and everything is beautiful in its time.

How do we do that? Think, ponder, pray, petition, write it down . . . go back to it, then live it out. My vision is to do a great job with my kids, and encourage the women God has put around me in my community. That won't happen overnight. I long for various projects to take off, but in the meantime about ten of us meet once a month in my front room to pray and read the Bible together. I know one of my biggest flaws is a lack of patience. But even though my timing is terrible, God's is perfect, and I know that I've got to continue to sow and serve while I wait.

I have often heard frustrated worship leaders complaining they are stuck in a coffee shop instead of on the stage. Or heard a passionate preacher frustrated by their lack of opportunity. What God tells us all is to be humble and patient, and embrace what it takes to get you there.

Remember David in the fields patiently watching the sheep? And Jesus himself was a carpenter for most of his adult life, faithfully getting ready for what God had in mind for him. He was thirty when his public ministry finally began. Sometimes the making of us is in the waiting. Growing and realising a dream can feel a little like watching the tide come in. Every time the waves get a little further in to the shore, they are pulled back out into the sea. This can go on and on for hours. It is sometimes tedious to watch. But if you look at the sand, more and more grains are being touched, soaked and covered each time.

It's easy to believe that having a big life is effortless for some people, but really it is a process of being patient and learning to persevere each time the waves knock us back; never doubting the progress and impact that each little splash forward is making, just like Mother Teresa so faithfully believed.

So do you want a big life? Maybe you are frustrated by the way things are, and the dreams that once burned brightly but now lie dormant. You want to make a difference, have an impact, and be used by God.

Just by praying that prayer, you are on the road. But it will be a long journey, full of many different stages and seasons. There is a time for everything and everything is beautiful in its time. Trust God, and don't become disillusioned by seasons of the ordinary. Work hard. Keep going. Be faithful. Be patient. You have made a beautiful choice!

10

Christ in you, the hope of glory

You've probably noticed by now that there's a whole lot of 'I wanna' going on in the chapter titles of this book: 'I wanna be an uncomplicated woman', 'I wanna have a big life', 'I wanna break the cycle'. But as I've tried to convey, these are not the vain cries of a comfort-loving, pampered life. These are the desperate and passionate prayers of a generation of women on a mission to become powerful tools in the hands of their God. There's not a hint here of the distorted 'I want . . .' declarations we hear swirling around us in today's self-obsessed and painfully broken society: 'I want to feel better about myself' or 'I want to be a powerful woman', or 'I want plastic surgery'. This is a more pure and more purposeful cry: 'I want to be a *woman of God*.'

Wanting to be an uncomplicated, free, affirmed and

empowered woman of God is a beautiful vision for life. But in order for it to become reality, we must move on from simply 'I' and take the all-important, final step. In this last chapter we focus on that missing piece. The Christian life is not you on your own, striving to make things happen by mere willpower, discipline or determination. Instead it is something far more glorious: 'Christ in you, the hope of glory' (Colossians 1:27).

As my Bible-teaching friend Louie Giglio often reminds people, it's not 'Christ and you, the hope of glory' – like some wrestling partnership, whereby every time you grow tired of the assaults, Jesus comes in to the ring to give you some recovery time, then hands everything back to you to try feebly again. It's not even just 'Christ with you'. He undoubtedly is with us – but too many of us have fallen for the 'God is my co-pilot' sticker campaign, where ultimately we're still in charge of the controls, and he's just giving us some incidental advice on navigating through this life. No, the beautiful news is this – it's 'Christ *in* you, the hope of glory'. The gloriously strong Maker and Sustainer of the universe is living in you – through the power of his Holy Spirit.

Think about that for a moment. The very same God

> The very same God who time after time led his people to win the day is living in and through *you*.

who time after time led his people to win the day is living in and through *you*. Who, through Moses, led the people of God out of slavery and into freedom. Who spoke powerfully through Deborah the prophetess. Who favoured the lives of Esther, Daniel and Joseph in their high-profile positions. Who gave strength to Samson and incredible victory to the shepherd boy David. Who performed powerful acts and miracles through the apostles and those who followed in their example. This very same God lives in *you* – continuously breathing his power in and through you to give birth to a godly life. Amazingly, the very same Holy Spirit of God who empowered Jesus for his perfect earthly ministry is now dwelling inside of you.

We live in a 'you can do it' generation. How often have you seen a pop star accepting an award, and pouring out their mantra of, 'You can achieve your dream. Just believe and keep following your heart' – forgetting, of course, to let you know that for every award-winning, chart-topping superstar, there are tens of thousands of 'also-rans' who never came anywhere near achieving such a dream.

The kingdom of God gives us a totally different idea of how to live the big life. Again and again the Bible reminds us that the power of God in us is what will bring success in the kingdom of God:

'Not by might nor by power, but by my Spirit,' says the Lord Almighty (Zechariah 4:6).

God chose the weak things of the world to shame the strong (1 Corinthians 1:27).

I delight in weaknesses . . . For when I am weak, then I am strong (2 Corinthians 12:10).

But he said to me, 'My grace is sufficient for you, for my power is made perfect in weakness.' Therefore I will boast all the more gladly about my weaknesses, so that Christ's power may rest on me (2 Corinthians 12:9).

The 'you can do it' generation say 'I can do everything . . .', but as women of God we complete the sentence: 'I can do everything through him who gives me strength' (Philippians 4:13).

In the last few decades society has taught women that strength and power must be fought for. Much of our culture has given a role model to young females that there are only two ways to liberation and status – either through aggression or seduction. The kingdom of God offers us a more pure and powerful way of being feminine and effective – Christ in our lives, the hope of glory. We surrender and he sustains us. We bow down, and he empowers us.

The first step is acknowledging our own feebleness. Human willpower may get you through one or two days of the victorious life, but before long you'll be back on your knees, where you first started. God has some beautiful ways of keeping us dependent on him. And that's a very good thing. Take a look through the Bible and you'll notice the people of God have a dangerous habit of losing their dependence when things are on a roll. As my wise friend Darlene Zschech explained it in the magazine *Worship Leader*:

> *Momentum can be your best friend. It's like the breath of God causing one day to be more valuable and worthwhile than a thousand . . . But you can abuse that momentum if you stop digging for the gold that gave you it in the first place. Momentum can give you a false sense of security . . . 'We can do it' . . . But at what cost? Before we know it, we've abused the privilege and lost sight of the higher call.*

If we're to live a big life, and be used powerfully in the kingdom of God, then reliance upon him will always be the key. As Oswald Chambers so wisely wrote in the daily devotional *My Utmost for His Highest*: 'Complete weakness and dependence will always be the occasion for the Spirit of God to manifest His power.'

I long to be part of a generation of young women who

recognise their complete weakness, but realise God's complete strength. Women who pursue a godly life, along with faith, love, perseverance and gentleness. Who fight the good fight, yet remain wholesomely feminine. A movement of young women who hold tightly to the things of God, and the eternal life he has given them, yet hold lightly to the things of this world. Women who care for one another and sharpen one another, setting an example for others by living out their daily lives overflowing with love, joy, faith, purity, peace, patience, kindness, goodness, faithfulness, gentleness and self-control. A generation of women who live by the Spirit, and keep in step with the Spirit.

So you wanna be a woman of God? Here's the stunning, glorious key: Christ in you, the hope of glory!

Mercy Ministries of America

Mercy Ministries of America is an international programme for girls and young women between the ages of thirteen and twenty-eight who are dealing with eating disorders, chemical addictions, unplanned pregnancies, abuse and other life-controlling problems. The girls must make an application to this free programme on a voluntary basis. A willing heart and sincere desire to change are prerequisites for entering the programme, and beginning the ultimate path to transformation.

During their six- to eight-month stay, girls receive care from trained professionals at the residential facilities completely free of charge. The daily schedule includes individual counselling, group counselling, life skills training, food and fitness instruction, medical care, academic instruction, and other components for ensuring a productive future.

The ultimate goal of Mercy Ministries is that every young woman who completes the Mercy programme becomes a law-abiding, tax-paying individual who is self-supporting with independent living skills, rather than depending on the government welfare system for support.

At Mercy, each girl's restoration process is unique according to the severity of her problems, but the approach to her restoration is the same – to promote spiritual stability by demonstrating and teaching the unconditional love and mercy of God, combined with the practical application and training for daily life.

For more information on becoming a financial partner to Mercy Ministries, or if you or someone you know needs Mercy, please visit the website at www.mercy ministries.com.

Also by Beth Redman:

Soul Sista

Ever get the feeling:

- you spend most of your life trying to be someone you don't really want to be?
- there are too many boys in the world, and not enough men?
- being a Christian shouldn't be half as difficult as everyone tells you it is?
- you want to know God, but you're not sure if he wants to know you?

It's time to fight back! *Soul Sista* is the definitive survival guide for every girl who's ever wondered why the holy life sometimes seems to be just one bad hair day after another. It's about becoming a Girl of God: proud to be a Christian, proud to be a woman.

Hodder & Stoughton
ISBN 0 340 75677 2

For the Audience of One

The Soul Survivor Guide to Worship

Mike Pilavachi with Craig Borlase

Worship is the reason for our existence but it's not about performing to the many. It is for God, the audience of one. We should be worshipping every minute of every day, and we don't need words or even a tune.

Soul Survivor is the heart of the incredible revival in contemporary youth worship. *For the Audience of One* shows that, beneath the surface level of words and music, a phenomenal work of God – anointed, culturally relevant and biblically sound – is taking place, enabling people to be broken, healed and transformed by him.

This book should be read by everyone with a desire to go deeper into worship, and includes a special section for worship leaders.

Hodder & Stoughton
ISBN 0 340 72190 1